THE MILLION DOLLAR

Gospel
of John

BBRIDGE
LLOGOS

Newberry, FL 32669

ONE MILLION DOLLARS

The Million Dollar Gospel of John
Commentary by Ray Comfort

Published by:
Bridge-Logos, Inc.
Newberry, FL 32669, USA
bridgelogos.com

ISBN 978-1-61036-267-2

Library of Congress Control Number: 2021936588

Edited by Lynn Copeland

Cover, page design, and production by Genesis Group, Inc. (genesis-group.net)

Printed in India

you from death's power, He can save you from the haunting fear of death that plagues every person. Please, today, repent and trust in Jesus alone, and God will forgive you and grant you the gift of everlasting life:

> For the wages of sin is death, but the gift of God is eternal life in Christ Jesus our Lord. (Romans 6:23)

Then, to show your gratitude to God for His amazing grace, read the Bible daily and obey what you read. Be sure to join a Christian church and be baptized. You can find information to help you grow in your faith at the bottom of the home page on LivingWaters.com.

Thank you for reading this introduction. Now, please take the time to read the amazing Gospel of John. Nothing is more valuable than your eternal salvation. For a summary of Jesus' unprecedented words and unparalleled works, be sure to read "The Uniqueness of Jesus" at the end of the booklet.

May God bless you.

Ray Comfort

*"For what profit is it to a man
if he gains the whole world,
and loses his own soul?
Or what will a man give in
exchange for his soul?"*

—Matthew 16:26

Preface
to the New King James Version®

The purpose of this most recent revision of the King James Version New Testament is in harmony with the purpose of the original King James scholars: "Not to make a new translation...but to make a good one better." The New King James Version is a continuation of the labors of the King James translators, unlocking for today's readers the spiritual treasures found especially in that version.

While seeking to maintain the excellent *form* of the traditional English New Testament, special care has also been taken to preserve the work of *precision* which is the legacy of the King James translators.

Where new translation has been necessary, the most complete representation of the original has been rendered by considering the definition and usage of the Greek words in their contexts. This translation principle, known as *complete equivalence*, seeks to preserve accurately all of the information in the text while presenting it in good literary form.

In addition to accuracy, the translators have also sought to maintain those lyrical and devotional qualities that are so highly regarded in the King James Version. The thought flow and selection of phrases from the King James Version have been preserved wherever possible without sacrificing clarity.

The format of the New King James Version is designed to enhance the vividness, devotional quality, and usefulness of the Bible. Words or phrases in italics indicate expressions in the original language that require clarification by additional English words, as was done in the King James Version. Oblique type in the New Testament indicates a quotation from the Old Testament. Poetry is structured as verse to reflect the form and beauty of the passage in the original language. The covenant name of God was usually translated from the Hebrew as LORD or GOD, using capital letters as shown, as in the King James Version. This convention is also maintained in the New King James Version when the Old Testament is quoted in the New.

The Hebrew text used for the Old Testament is the 1967/1977 Stuttgart edition of the *Biblia Hebraica*, with frequent comparisons to the Bomberg edition of 1524-25. Ancient versions and the Dead Sea Scrolls were consulted, but the Hebrew is followed wherever possible. Significant variations, explanations, and alternate renderings are mentioned in footnotes.

The Greek text used for the New Testament is the one that was followed by the King James translators: the traditional text of the Greek-speaking churches, called the Received Text or Textus Receptus, first published in 1516. Footnotes indicate significant variants from the Textus Receptus as found in two other editions of the Greek New Testament:

(1) NU-Text: These variations generally represent the Alexandrian or Egyptian text type as found in the critical text published in the twenty-sixth edition of the Nestle-Aland Greek New Testament (N) and in the United Bible Societies' third edition (U).

(2) M-Text: These variations represent readings found in the text of the first edition of *The Greek New Testament According to the Majority Text*, which follows the consensus of the majority of surviving New Testament manuscripts.

The textual notes in the New King James Version make no evaluation, but objectively present the facts about variant readings.

John

The Eternal Word

1 In the beginning was the Word, and the Word was with God, and the Word was God. [2]He was in the beginning with God. [3]All things were made through Him, and without Him nothing was made that was made. [4]In Him was life, and the life was the light of men. [5]And the light shines in the darkness, and the darkness did not comprehend[a] it.

John's Witness: The True Light

[6]There was a man sent from God, whose name *was* John. [7]This man came for a witness, to bear witness of the Light, that all through him might believe. [8]He was not that Light, but *was sent* to bear witness of that Light. [9]That was the true Light which gives light to every man coming into the world.[a]

[10]He was in the world, and the world was made through Him, and the world did not know Him. [11]He came to His own,[a] and His own[b] did not receive Him. [12]But as many as received Him, to them He gave the right to become children of God, to those who believe in His name: [13]who were born,

---

1:5 [a]Or *overcome* 1:9 [a]Or *That was the true Light which, coming into the world, gives light to every man.* 1:11 [a]That is, His own things or domain [b]That is, His own people

not of blood, nor of the will of the flesh, nor of the will of man, but of God.

The Word Becomes Flesh

[14]And the Word became flesh and dwelt among us, and we beheld His glory, the glory as of the only begotten of the Father, full of grace and truth.

[15]John bore witness of Him and cried out, saying, "This was He of whom I said, 'He who comes after me is preferred before me, for He was before me.' "

[16]And[a] of His fullness we have all received, and grace for grace. [17]For the law was given through Moses, *but* grace and truth came through Jesus Christ. [18]No one has seen God at any time. The only begotten Son,[a] who is in the bosom of the Father, He has declared *Him*.

A Voice in the Wilderness

[19]Now this is the testimony of John, when the Jews sent priests and Levites from Jerusalem to ask him, "Who are you?"

[20]He confessed, and did not deny, but confessed, "I am not the Christ."

[21]And they asked him, "What then? Are you Elijah?"

He said, "I am not."

"Are you the Prophet?"

And he answered, "No."

[22]Then they said to him, "Who are

1:16 [a]NU-Text reads *For.*   1:18 [a]NU-Text reads *only begotten God.*

you, that we may give an answer to those who sent us? What do you say about yourself?"

[23]He said: "I *am*

> *The voice of one crying in the wilderness:*
> "*Make straight the way of the Lord,*" '[a]

as the prophet Isaiah said."

[24]Now those who were sent were from the Pharisees. [25]And they asked him, saying, "Why then do you baptize if you are not the Christ, nor Elijah, nor the Prophet?"

[26]John answered them, saying, "I baptize with water, but there stands One among you whom you do not know. [27]It is He who, coming after me, is preferred before me, whose sandal strap I am not worthy to loose."

[28]These things were done in Bethabara[a] beyond the Jordan, where John was baptizing.

The Lamb of God

[29]The next day John saw Jesus coming toward him, and said, "Behold! The Lamb of God who takes away the sin of the world! [30]This is He of whom I said, 'After me comes a Man who is preferred before me, for He was before me.' [31]I did not know Him; but that He should be revealed to Israel, therefore I came baptizing with water."

[32]And John bore witness, saying, "I

1:23 [a]Isaiah 40:3   1:28 [a]NU-Text and M-Text read *Bethany*.

saw the Spirit descending from heaven like a dove, and He remained upon Him. [33]I did not know Him, but He who sent me to baptize with water said to me, 'Upon whom you see the Spirit descending, and remaining on Him, this is He who baptizes with the Holy Spirit.' [34]And I have seen and testified that this is the Son of God."

The First Disciples

[35]Again, the next day, John stood with two of his disciples. [36]And looking at Jesus as He walked, he said, "Behold the Lamb of God!"

[37]The two disciples heard him speak, and they followed Jesus. [38]Then Jesus turned, and seeing them following, said to them, "What do you seek?"

They said to Him, "Rabbi" (which is to say, when translated, Teacher), "where are You staying?"

[39]He said to them, "Come and see." They came and saw where He was staying, and remained with Him that day (now it was about the tenth hour).

[40]One of the two who heard John *speak,* and followed Him, was Andrew, Simon Peter's brother. [41]He first found his own brother Simon, and said to him, "We have found the Messiah" (which is translated, the Christ). [42]And he brought him to Jesus.

Now when Jesus looked at him, He said, "You are Simon the son of Jonah.[a] You shall be called Cephas" (which is

1:42 [a]NU-Text reads *John.*

translated, A Stone).

Philip and Nathanael

⁴³The following day Jesus wanted to go to Galilee, and He found Philip and said to him, "Follow Me." ⁴⁴Now Philip was from Bethsaida, the city of Andrew and Peter. ⁴⁵Philip found Nathanael and said to him, "We have found Him of whom Moses in the law, and also the prophets, wrote—Jesus of Nazareth, the son of Joseph."

⁴⁶And Nathanael said to him, "Can anything good come out of Nazareth?"

Philip said to him, "Come and see."

⁴⁷Jesus saw Nathanael coming toward Him, and said of him, "Behold, an Israelite indeed, in whom is no deceit!"

⁴⁸Nathanael said to Him, "How do You know me?"

Jesus answered and said to him, "Before Philip called you, when you were under the fig tree, I saw you."

⁴⁹Nathanael answered and said to Him, "Rabbi, You are the Son of God! You are the King of Israel!"

⁵⁰Jesus answered and said to him, "Because I said to you, 'I saw you under the fig tree,' do you believe? You will see greater things than these." ⁵¹And He said to him, "Most assuredly, I say to you, hereafter[a] you shall see heaven open, and the angels of God ascending and descending upon the Son of Man."

1:51 [a]NU-Text omits *hereafter*.

Water Turned to Wine

2 On the third day there was a wedding in Cana of Galilee, and the mother of Jesus was there. [2]Now both Jesus and His disciples were invited to the wedding. [3]And when they ran out of wine, the mother of Jesus said to Him, "They have no wine."

[4]Jesus said to her, "Woman, what does your concern have to do with Me? My hour has not yet come."

[5]His mother said to the servants, "Whatever He says to you, do *it*."

[6]Now there were set there six waterpots of stone, according to the manner of purification of the Jews, containing twenty or thirty gallons apiece. [7]Jesus said to them, "Fill the waterpots with water." And they filled them up to the brim. [8]And He said to them, "Draw *some* out now, and take *it* to the master of the feast." And they took *it*. [9]When the master of the feast had tasted the water that was made wine, and did not know where it came from (but the servants who had drawn the water knew), the master of the feast called the bridegroom. [10]And he said to him, "Every man at the beginning sets out the good wine, and when the *guests* have well drunk, then the inferior. You have kept the good wine until now!"

[11]This beginning of signs Jesus did in Cana of Galilee, and manifested His glory; and His disciples believed in Him.

¹²After this He went down to Capernaum, He, His mother, His brothers, and His disciples; and they did not stay there many days.

Jesus Cleanses the Temple

¹³Now the Passover of the Jews was at hand, and Jesus went up to Jerusalem. ¹⁴And He found in the temple those who sold oxen and sheep and doves, and the money changers doing business. ¹⁵When He had made a whip of cords, He drove them all out of the temple, with the sheep and the oxen, and poured out the changers' money and overturned the tables. ¹⁶And He said to those who sold doves, "Take these things away! Do not make My Father's house a house of merchandise!" ¹⁷Then His disciples remembered that it was written, *"Zeal for Your house has eaten*[a] *Me up."*[b]

¹⁸So the Jews answered and said to Him, "What sign do You show to us, since You do these things?"

¹⁹Jesus answered and said to them, "Destroy this temple, and in three days I will raise it up."

²⁰Then the Jews said, "It has taken forty-six years to build this temple, and will You raise it up in three days?"

²¹But He was speaking of the temple of His body. ²²Therefore, when He had risen from the dead, His disciples remembered that He had said this to

---

2:17 [a]NU-Text and M-Text read *will eat.* [b]Psalm 69:9

them;[a] and they believed the Scripture and the word which Jesus had said.

The Discerner of Hearts

[23]Now when He was in Jerusalem at the Passover, during the feast, many believed in His name when they saw the signs which He did. [24]But Jesus did not commit Himself to them, because He knew all *men,* [25]and had no need that anyone should testify of man, for He knew what was in man.

The New Birth

3 There was a man of the Pharisees named Nicodemus, a ruler of the Jews. [2]This man came to Jesus by night and said to Him, "Rabbi, we know that You are a teacher come from God; for no one can do these signs that You do unless God is with him."

[3]Jesus answered and said to him, "Most assuredly, I say to you, unless one is born again, he cannot see the kingdom of God."

[4]Nicodemus said to Him, "How can a man be born when he is old? Can he enter a second time into his mother's womb and be born?"

[5]Jesus answered, "Most assuredly, I say to you, unless one is born of water and the Spirit, he cannot enter the kingdom of God. [6]That which is born of the flesh is flesh, and that which is born of the Spirit is spirit. [7]Do not

---

2:22 [a]NU-Text and M-Text omit *to them.*

marvel that I said to you, 'You must be born again.' [8]The wind blows where it wishes, and you hear the sound of it, but cannot tell where it comes from and where it goes. So is everyone who is born of the Spirit."

[9]Nicodemus answered and said to Him, "How can these things be?"

[10]Jesus answered and said to him, "Are you the teacher of Israel, and do not know these things? [11]Most assuredly, I say to you, We speak what We know and testify what We have seen, and you do not receive Our witness. [12]If I have told you earthly things and you do not believe, how will you believe if I tell you heavenly things? [13]No one has ascended to heaven but He who came down from heaven, *that is,* the Son of Man who is in heaven.[a] [14]And as Moses lifted up the serpent in the wilderness, even so must the Son of Man be lifted up, [15]that whoever believes in Him should not perish but[a] have eternal life. [16]For God so loved the world that He gave His only begotten Son, that whoever believes in Him should not perish but have everlasting life. [17]For God did not send His Son into the world to condemn the world, but that the world through Him might be saved.

[18]"He who believes in Him is not condemned; but he who does not believe is condemned already, because he

---

3:13 [a]NU-Text omits *who is in heaven.*   3:15 [a]NU-Text omits *not perish but.*

has not believed in the name of the only begotten Son of God. ¹⁹And this is the condemnation, that the light has come into the world, and men loved darkness rather than light, because their deeds were evil. ²⁰For everyone practicing evil hates the light and does not come to the light, lest his deeds should be exposed. ²¹But he who does the truth comes to the light, that his deeds may be clearly seen, that they have been done in God."

John the Baptist Exalts Christ

²²After these things Jesus and His disciples came into the land of Judea, and there He remained with them and baptized. ²³Now John also was baptizing in Aenon near Salim, because there was much water there. And they came and were baptized. ²⁴For John had not yet been thrown into prison.

²⁵Then there arose a dispute between *some* of John's disciples and the Jews about purification. ²⁶And they came to John and said to him, "Rabbi, He who was with you beyond the Jordan, to whom you have testified—behold, He is baptizing, and all are coming to Him!"

²⁷John answered and said, "A man can receive nothing unless it has been given to him from heaven. ²⁸You yourselves bear me witness, that I said, 'I am not the Christ,' but, 'I have been sent before Him.' ²⁹He who has the bride is the bridegroom; but the friend

of the bridegroom, who stands and hears him, rejoices greatly because of the bridegroom's voice. Therefore this joy of mine is fulfilled. [30]He must increase, but I *must* decrease. [31]He who comes from above is above all; he who is of the earth is earthly and speaks of the earth. He who comes from heaven is above all. [32]And what He has seen and heard, that He testifies; and no one receives His testimony. [33]He who has received His testimony has certified that God is true. [34]For He whom God has sent speaks the words of God, for God does not give the Spirit by measure. [35]The Father loves the Son, and has given all things into His hand. [36]He who believes in the Son has everlasting life; and he who does not believe the Son shall not see life, but the wrath of God abides on him."

A Samaritan Woman Meets Her Messiah

4 Therefore, when the Lord knew that the Pharisees had heard that Jesus made and baptized more disciples than John [2](though Jesus Himself did not baptize, but His disciples), [3]He left Judea and departed again to Galilee. [4]But He needed to go through Samaria.

[5]So He came to a city of Samaria which is called Sychar, near the plot of ground that Jacob gave to his son Joseph. [6]Now Jacob's well was there. Jesus therefore, being wearied from *His* journey, sat thus by the well. It was

about the sixth hour.

⁷A woman of Samaria came to draw water. Jesus said to her, "Give Me a drink." ⁸For His disciples had gone away into the city to buy food.

⁹Then the woman of Samaria said to Him, "How is it that You, being a Jew, ask a drink from me, a Samaritan woman?" For Jews have no dealings with Samaritans.

¹⁰Jesus answered and said to her, "If you knew the gift of God, and who it is who says to you, 'Give Me a drink,' you would have asked Him, and He would have given you living water."

¹¹The woman said to Him, "Sir, You have nothing to draw with, and the well is deep. Where then do You get that living water? ¹²Are You greater than our father Jacob, who gave us the well, and drank from it himself, as well as his sons and his livestock?"

¹³Jesus answered and said to her, "Whoever drinks of this water will thirst again, ¹⁴but whoever drinks of the water that I shall give him will never thirst. But the water that I shall give him will become in him a fountain of water springing up into everlasting life."

¹⁵The woman said to Him, "Sir, give me this water, that I may not thirst, nor come here to draw."

¹⁶Jesus said to her, "Go, call your husband, and come here."

¹⁷The woman answered and said, "I have no husband."

Jesus said to her, "You have well said, 'I have no husband,' [18]for you have had five husbands, and the one whom you now have is not your husband; in that you spoke truly."

[19]The woman said to Him, "Sir, I perceive that You are a prophet. [20]Our fathers worshiped on this mountain, and you *Jews* say that in Jerusalem is the place where one ought to worship."

[21]Jesus said to her, "Woman, believe Me, the hour is coming when you will neither on this mountain, nor in Jerusalem, worship the Father. [22]You worship what you do not know; we know what we worship, for salvation is of the Jews. [23]But the hour is coming, and now is, when the true worshipers will worship the Father in spirit and truth; for the Father is seeking such to worship Him. [24]God *is* Spirit, and those who worship Him must worship in spirit and truth."

[25]The woman said to Him, "I know that Messiah is coming" (who is called Christ). "When He comes, He will tell us all things."

[26]Jesus said to her, "I who speak to you am *He*."

The Whitened Harvest

[27]And at this *point* His disciples came, and they marveled that He talked with a woman; yet no one said, "What do You seek?" or, "Why are You talking with her?"

[28]The woman then left her water-

pot, went her way into the city, and said to the men, [29]"Come, see a Man who told me all things that I ever did. Could this be the Christ?" [30]Then they went out of the city and came to Him.

[31]In the meantime His disciples urged Him, saying, "Rabbi, eat."

[32]But He said to them, "I have food to eat of which you do not know."

[33]Therefore the disciples said to one another, "Has anyone brought Him *anything* to eat?"

[34]Jesus said to them, "My food is to do the will of Him who sent Me, and to finish His work. [35]Do you not say, 'There are still four months and *then* comes the harvest'? Behold, I say to you, lift up your eyes and look at the fields, for they are already white for harvest! [36]And he who reaps receives wages, and gathers fruit for eternal life, that both he who sows and he who reaps may rejoice together. [37]For in this the saying is true: 'One sows and another reaps.' [38]I sent you to reap that for which you have not labored; others have labored, and you have entered into their labors."

The Savior of the World

[39]And many of the Samaritans of that city believed in Him because of the word of the woman who testified, "He told me all that I *ever* did." [40]So when the Samaritans had come to Him, they urged Him to stay with them; and He stayed there two days. [41]And many more

and that believing you may have life
in His name. (John 20:30,31)

In the Old Testament God promised
to destroy humanity's greatest enemy—
death itself. The New Testament tells us
exactly how He did it.

Let me briefly share with you what
He did by asking if you think you are a
good person. Are you good enough to
make it to Heaven? To find out, let's look
at the Ten Commandments. Have you
ever lied, stolen anything, used God's
name in vain, or lusted in your heart for
another person? Jesus said that to lust is
to commit adultery:

> "You have heard that it was said to
> those of old, 'You shall not commit
> adultery.' But I say to you that who-
> ever looks at a woman to lust for her
> has already committed adultery with
> her in his heart." (Matthew 5:27,28)

If you have broken those Commandments, God sees you as a liar, a thief, a
blasphemer, and an adulterer at heart.
The penalty for sin is death, and if you die
in your sins, you will end up in a terrible
place called Hell. *Please don't let that
happen.*

Here is the good news of the gospel:
Though we broke God's moral Law, Jesus
paid the fine by suffering and dying on
the cross: "God so loved the world that
He gave His only begotten Son, that whoever believes in Him should not perish
but have everlasting life" (John 3:16).
Then Jesus rose from the dead and de-
feated death. Today, He can not only save

Introduction

Thank you for opening this publication. First, let me explain why we have a million dollar bill on the cover. A young man found that when his grandmother died, she had left him $20,000 as well as "my Bible and all it contains." He didn't bother to open the Bible but put it on a high shelf, gambled the $20,000, and over the next fifty years he made just enough to scrape by.

One day, as he moved that dusty old Bible, it fell and opened to reveal money between every page—a total of one million dollars. He could have lived his life in luxury, but didn't because he thought he knew what the Bible contained.

You hold in your hands a small portion of the best-selling Book of all time. The Bible contains something far more valuable than a mere one million dollars. It tells us how to find the riches of everlasting life and answers the million-dollar question: *Where will I go when I die?*

The Gospel of John is an eyewitness account of Jesus of Nazareth, whose life was so impactful that our BC/AD calendar marks His birth as the dividing point of history. This Gospel ("good news") can give you the answer to that most important question. A closing chapter ends by saying,

> And truly Jesus did many other signs in the presence of His disciples, which are not written in this book; but these are written that you may believe that Jesus is the Christ, the Son of God,

believed because of His own word.

⁴²Then they said to the woman, "Now we believe, not because of what you said, for we ourselves have heard *Him* and we know that this is indeed the Christ,[a] the Savior of the world."

Welcome at Galilee

⁴³Now after the two days He departed from there and went to Galilee. ⁴⁴For Jesus Himself testified that a prophet has no honor in his own country. ⁴⁵So when He came to Galilee, the Galileans received Him, having seen all the things He did in Jerusalem at the feast; for they also had gone to the feast.

A Nobleman's Son Healed

⁴⁶So Jesus came again to Cana of Galilee where He had made the water wine. And there was a certain nobleman whose son was sick at Capernaum. ⁴⁷When he heard that Jesus had come out of Judea into Galilee, he went to Him and implored Him to come down and heal his son, for he was at the point of death. ⁴⁸Then Jesus said to him, "Unless you *people* see signs and wonders, you will by no means believe."

⁴⁹The nobleman said to Him, "Sir, come down before my child dies!"

⁵⁰Jesus said to him, "Go your way; your son lives." So the man believed the word that Jesus spoke to him, and

---

4:42 [a]NU-Text omits *the Christ*.

he went his way. [51]And as he was now going down, his servants met him and told *him,* saying, "Your son lives!"

[52]Then he inquired of them the hour when he got better. And they said to him, "Yesterday at the seventh hour the fever left him." [53]So the father knew that *it was* at the same hour in which Jesus said to him, "Your son lives." And he himself believed, and his whole household.

[54]This again *is* the second sign Jesus did when He had come out of Judea into Galilee.

A Man Healed at the Pool of Bethesda

5 After this there was a feast of the Jews, and Jesus went up to Jerusalem. [2]Now there is in Jerusalem by the Sheep *Gate* a pool, which is called in Hebrew, Bethesda,[a] having five porches. [3]In these lay a great multitude of sick people, blind, lame, paralyzed, waiting for the moving of the water. [4]For an angel went down at a certain time into the pool and stirred up the water; then whoever stepped in first, after the stirring of the water, was made well of whatever disease he had.[a] [5]Now a certain man was there who had an infirmity thirty-eight years. [6]When Jesus saw him lying there, and knew that he already had been *in that condition* a long

---

5:2 [a]NU-Text reads *Bethzatha.*   5:4 [a]NU-Text omits *waiting for the moving of the water* at the end of verse 3, and all of verse 4.

time, He said to him, "Do you want to be made well?"

⁷The sick man answered Him, "Sir, I have no man to put me into the pool when the water is stirred up; but while I am coming, another steps down before me."

⁸Jesus said to him, "Rise, take up your bed and walk." ⁹And immediately the man was made well, took up his bed, and walked.

And that day was the Sabbath. ¹⁰The Jews therefore said to him who was cured, "It is the Sabbath; it is not lawful for you to carry your bed."

¹¹He answered them, "He who made me well said to me, 'Take up your bed and walk.' "

¹²Then they asked him, "Who is the Man who said to you, 'Take up your bed and walk'?" ¹³But the one who was healed did not know who it was, for Jesus had withdrawn, a multitude being in *that* place. ¹⁴Afterward Jesus found him in the temple, and said to him, "See, you have been made well. Sin no more, lest a worse thing come upon you."

¹⁵The man departed and told the Jews that it was Jesus who had made him well.

Honor the Father and the Son

¹⁶For this reason the Jews persecuted Jesus, and sought to kill Him,ᵃ because He had done these things on

5:16 ᵃNU-Text omits *and sought to kill Him*.

the Sabbath. [17]But Jesus answered them, "My Father has been working until now, and I have been working."

[18]Therefore the Jews sought all the more to kill Him, because He not only broke the Sabbath, but also said that God was His Father, making Himself equal with God. [19]Then Jesus answered and said to them, "Most assuredly, I say to you, the Son can do nothing of Himself, but what He sees the Father do; for whatever He does, the Son also does in like manner. [20]For the Father loves the Son, and shows Him all things that He Himself does; and He will show Him greater works than these, that you may marvel. [21]For as the Father raises the dead and gives life to *them,* even so the Son gives life to whom He will. [22]For the Father judges no one, but has committed all judgment to the Son, [23]that all should honor the Son just as they honor the Father. He who does not honor the Son does not honor the Father who sent Him.

Life and Judgment Are Through the Son

[24]"Most assuredly, I say to you, he who hears My word and believes in Him who sent Me has everlasting life, and shall not come into judgment, but has passed from death into life. [25]Most assuredly, I say to you, the hour is coming, and now is, when the dead

will hear the voice of the Son of God; and those who hear will live. [26]For as the Father has life in Himself, so He has granted the Son to have life in Himself, [27]and has given Him authority to execute judgment also, because He is the Son of Man. [28]Do not marvel at this; for the hour is coming in which all who are in the graves will hear His voice [29]and come forth—those who have done good, to the resurrection of life, and those who have done evil, to the resurrection of condemnation. [30]I can of Myself do nothing. As I hear, I judge; and My judgment is righteous, because I do not seek My own will but the will of the Father who sent Me.

The Fourfold Witness

[31]"If I bear witness of Myself, My witness is not true. [32]There is another who bears witness of Me, and I know that the witness which He witnesses of Me is true. [33]You have sent to John, and he has borne witness to the truth. [34]Yet I do not receive testimony from man, but I say these things that you may be saved. [35]He was the burning and shining lamp, and you were willing for a time to rejoice in his light. [36]But I have a greater witness than John's; for the works which the Father has given Me to finish—the very works that I do—bear witness of Me, that the Father has sent Me. [37]And the Father Himself, who sent Me, has testified of Me.

You have neither heard His voice at any time, nor seen His form. ³⁸But you do not have His word abiding in you, because whom He sent, Him you do not believe. ³⁹You search the Scriptures, for in them you think you have eternal life; and these are they which testify of Me. ⁴⁰But you are not willing to come to Me that you may have life.

⁴¹"I do not receive honor from men. ⁴²But I know you, that you do not have the love of God in you. ⁴³I have come in My Father's name, and you do not receive Me; if another comes in his own name, him you will receive. ⁴⁴How can you believe, who receive honor from one another, and do not seek the honor that *comes* from the only God? ⁴⁵Do not think that I shall accuse you to the Father; there is *one* who accuses you— Moses, in whom you trust. ⁴⁶For if you believed Moses, you would believe Me; for he wrote about Me. ⁴⁷But if you do not believe his writings, how will you believe My words?"

Feeding the Five Thousand

6 After these things Jesus went over the Sea of Galilee, which is *the Sea* of Tiberias. ²Then a great multitude followed Him, because they saw His signs which He performed on those who were diseased. ³And Jesus went up on the mountain, and there He sat with His disciples. ⁴Now the Passover, a feast of the

Jews, was near. [5]Then Jesus lifted up *His* eyes, and seeing a great multitude coming toward Him, He said to Philip, "Where shall we buy bread, that these may eat?" [6]But this He said to test him, for He Himself knew what He would do.

[7]Philip answered Him, "Two hundred denarii worth of bread is not sufficient for them, that every one of them may have a little."

[8]One of His disciples, Andrew, Simon Peter's brother, said to Him, [9]"There is a lad here who has five barley loaves and two small fish, but what are they among so many?"

[10]Then Jesus said, "Make the people sit down." Now there was much grass in the place. So the men sat down, in number about five thousand. [11]And Jesus took the loaves, and when He had given thanks He distributed *them* to the disciples, and the disciples[a] to those sitting down; and likewise of the fish, as much as they wanted. [12]So when they were filled, He said to His disciples, "Gather up the fragments that remain, so that nothing is lost." [13]Therefore they gathered *them* up, and filled twelve baskets with the fragments of the five barley loaves which were left over by those who had eaten. [14]Then those men, when they had seen the sign that Jesus did, said, "This is truly the Prophet who is to come into the world."

6:11 [a]NU-Text omits *to the disciples, and the disciples.*

Jesus Walks on the Sea

[15]Therefore when Jesus perceived that they were about to come and take Him by force to make Him king, He departed again to the mountain by Himself alone.

[16]Now when evening came, His disciples went down to the sea, [17]got into the boat, and went over the sea toward Capernaum. And it was already dark, and Jesus had not come to them. [18]Then the sea arose because a great wind was blowing. [19]So when they had rowed about three or four miles,[a] they saw Jesus walking on the sea and drawing near the boat; and they were afraid. [20]But He said to them, "It is I; do not be afraid." [21]Then they willingly received Him into the boat, and immediately the boat was at the land where they were going.

The Bread from Heaven

[22]On the following day, when the people who were standing on the other side of the sea saw that there was no other boat there, except that one which His disciples had entered,[a] and that Jesus had not entered the boat with His disciples, but His disciples had gone away alone— [23]however, other boats came from Tiberias, near the place where they ate bread after the Lord had given thanks— [24]when the people therefore saw that Jesus was not there, nor

6:19 [a]Literally twenty-five or thirty stadia   6:22 [a]NU-Text omits that and which His disciples had entered.

His disciples, they also got into boats and came to Capernaum, seeking Jesus. ²⁵And when they found Him on the other side of the sea, they said to Him, "Rabbi, when did You come here?"

²⁶Jesus answered them and said, "Most assuredly, I say to you, you seek Me, not because you saw the signs, but because you ate of the loaves and were filled. ²⁷Do not labor for the food which perishes, but for the food which endures to everlasting life, which the Son of Man will give you, because God the Father has set His seal on Him."

²⁸Then they said to Him, "What shall we do, that we may work the works of God?"

²⁹Jesus answered and said to them, "This is the work of God, that you believe in Him whom He sent."

³⁰Therefore they said to Him, "What sign will You perform then, that we may see it and believe You? What work will You do? ³¹Our fathers ate the manna in the desert; as it is written, *'He gave them bread from heaven to eat.'* "ᵃ

³²Then Jesus said to them, "Most assuredly, I say to you, Moses did not give you the bread from heaven, but My Father gives you the true bread from heaven. ³³For the bread of God is He who comes down from heaven and gives life to the world."

³⁴Then they said to Him, "Lord, give us this bread always."

³⁵And Jesus said to them, "I am the

6:31 ᵃExodus 16:4; Nehemiah 9:15; Psalm 78:24

bread of life. He who comes to Me shall never hunger, and he who believes in Me shall never thirst. [36]But I said to you that you have seen Me and yet do not believe. [37]All that the Father gives Me will come to Me, and the one who comes to Me I will by no means cast out. [38]For I have come down from heaven, not to do My own will, but the will of Him who sent Me. [39]This is the will of the Father who sent Me, that of all He has given Me I should lose nothing, but should raise it up at the last day. [40]And this is the will of Him who sent Me, that everyone who sees the Son and believes in Him may have everlasting life; and I will raise him up at the last day."

Rejected by His Own

[41]The Jews then complained about Him, because He said, "I am the bread which came down from heaven." [42]And they said, "Is not this Jesus, the son of Joseph, whose father and mother we know? How is it then that He says, 'I have come down from heaven'?"

[43]Jesus therefore answered and said to them, "Do not murmur among yourselves. [44]No one can come to Me unless the Father who sent Me draws him; and I will raise him up at the last day. [45]It is written in the prophets, *'And they shall all be taught by God.'*[a] Therefore everyone who has heard and learned[b] from the Father comes to Me.

6:45 [a]Isaiah 54:13 [b]M-Text reads *hears and has learned.*

⁴⁶Not that anyone has seen the Father, except He who is from God; He has seen the Father. ⁴⁷Most assuredly, I say to you, he who believes in Me[a] has everlasting life. ⁴⁸I am the bread of life. ⁴⁹Your fathers ate the manna in the wilderness, and are dead. ⁵⁰This is the bread which comes down from heaven, that one may eat of it and not die. ⁵¹I am the living bread which came down from heaven. If anyone eats of this bread, he will live forever; and the bread that I shall give is My flesh, which I shall give for the life of the world."

⁵²The Jews therefore quarreled among themselves, saying, "How can this Man give us *His* flesh to eat?"

⁵³Then Jesus said to them, "Most assuredly, I say to you, unless you eat the flesh of the Son of Man and drink His blood, you have no life in you. ⁵⁴Whoever eats My flesh and drinks My blood has eternal life, and I will raise him up at the last day. ⁵⁵For My flesh is food indeed,[a] and My blood is drink indeed. ⁵⁶He who eats My flesh and drinks My blood abides in Me, and I in him. ⁵⁷As the living Father sent Me, and I live because of the Father, so he who feeds on Me will live because of Me. ⁵⁸This is the bread which came down from heaven—not as your fathers ate the manna, and are dead. He who eats this bread will live forever."

6:47 [a]NU-Text omits *in Me.* 6:55 [a]NU-Text reads *true food* and *true drink.*

[59]These things He said in the synagogue as He taught in Capernaum.

Many Disciples Turn Away

[60]Therefore many of His disciples, when they heard *this,* said, "This is a hard saying; who can understand it?" [61]When Jesus knew in Himself that His disciples complained about this, He said to them, "Does this offend you? [62]*What* then if you should see the Son of Man ascend where He was before? [63]It is the Spirit who gives life; the flesh profits nothing. The words that I speak to you are spirit, and *they* are life. [64]But there are some of you who do not believe." For Jesus knew from the beginning who they were who did not believe, and who would betray Him. [65]And He said, "Therefore I have said to you that no one can come to Me unless it has been granted to him by My Father."

[66]From that *time* many of His disciples went back and walked with Him no more. [67]Then Jesus said to the twelve, "Do you also want to go away?"

[68]But Simon Peter answered Him, "Lord, to whom shall we go? You have the words of eternal life. [69]Also we have come to believe and know that You are the Christ, the Son of the living God."[a]

[70]Jesus answered them, "Did I not choose you, the twelve, and one of you is a devil?" [71]He spoke of Judas Iscariot,

---

6:69 [a]NU-Text reads *You are the Holy One of God.*

the son of Simon, for it was he who would betray Him, being one of the twelve.

Jesus' Brothers Disbelieve

7 After these things Jesus walked in Galilee; for He did not want to walk in Judea, because the Jews[a] sought to kill Him. [2]Now the Jews' Feast of Tabernacles was at hand. [3]His brothers therefore said to Him, "Depart from here and go into Judea, that Your disciples also may see the works that You are doing. [4]For no one does anything in secret while he himself seeks to be known openly. If You do these things, show Yourself to the world." [5]For even His brothers did not believe in Him.

[6]Then Jesus said to them, "My time has not yet come, but your time is always ready. [7]The world cannot hate you, but it hates Me because I testify of it that its works are evil. [8]You go up to this feast. I am not yet[a] going up to this feast, for My time has not yet fully come." [9]When He had said these things to them, He remained in Galilee.

The Heavenly Scholar

[10]But when His brothers had gone up, then He also went up to the feast, not openly, but as it were in secret. [11]Then the Jews sought Him at the feast, and said, "Where is He?" [12]And there was much complaining among

---

7:1 [a]That is, the ruling authorities   7:8 [a]NU-Text omits *yet*.

the people concerning Him. Some said, "He is good"; others said, "No, on the contrary, He deceives the people." ¹³However, no one spoke openly of Him for fear of the Jews.

¹⁴Now about the middle of the feast Jesus went up into the temple and taught. ¹⁵And the Jews marveled, saying, "How does this Man know letters, having never studied?"

¹⁶Jesus[a] answered them and said, "My doctrine is not Mine, but His who sent Me. ¹⁷If anyone wills to do His will, he shall know concerning the doctrine, whether it is from God or *whether* I speak on My own *authority*. ¹⁸He who speaks from himself seeks his own glory; but He who seeks the glory of the One who sent Him is true, and no unrighteousness is in Him. ¹⁹Did not Moses give you the law, yet none of you keeps the law? Why do you seek to kill Me?"

²⁰The people answered and said, "You have a demon. Who is seeking to kill You?"

²¹Jesus answered and said to them, "I did one work, and you all marvel. ²²Moses therefore gave you circumcision (not that it is from Moses, but from the fathers), and you circumcise a man on the Sabbath. ²³If a man receives circumcision on the Sabbath, so that the law of Moses should not be broken, are you angry with Me because

---

7:16 ᵃNU-Text and M-Text read *So Jesus*.

I made a man completely well on the Sabbath? [24]Do not judge according to appearance, but judge with righteous judgment."

Could This Be the Christ?

[25]Now some of them from Jerusalem said, "Is this not He whom they seek to kill? [26]But look! He speaks boldly, and they say nothing to Him. Do the rulers know indeed that this is truly[a] the Christ? [27]However, we know where this Man is from; but when the Christ comes, no one knows where He is from."

[28]Then Jesus cried out, as He taught in the temple, saying, "You both know Me, and you know where I am from; and I have not come of Myself, but He who sent Me is true, whom you do not know. [29]But[a] I know Him, for I am from Him, and He sent Me."

[30]Therefore they sought to take Him; but no one laid a hand on Him, because His hour had not yet come. [31]And many of the people believed in Him, and said, "When the Christ comes, will He do more signs than these which this *Man* has done?"

Jesus and the Religious Leaders

[32]The Pharisees heard the crowd murmuring these things concerning Him, and the Pharisees and the chief priests sent officers to take Him.

7:26 [a]NU-Text omits *truly*. 7:29 [a]NU-Text and M-Text omit *But*.

[33]Then Jesus said to them,[a] "I shall be with you a little while longer, and *then* I go to Him who sent Me. [34]You will seek Me and not find *Me,* and where I am you cannot come."

[35]Then the Jews said among themselves, "Where does He intend to go that we shall not find Him? Does He intend to go to the Dispersion among the Greeks and teach the Greeks? [36]What is this thing that He said, 'You will seek Me and not find Me, and where I am you cannot come'?"

The Promise of the Holy Spirit

[37]On the last day, that great *day* of the feast, Jesus stood and cried out, saying, "If anyone thirsts, let him come to Me and drink. [38]He who believes in Me, as the Scripture has said, out of his heart will flow rivers of living water." [39]But this He spoke concerning the Spirit, whom those believing[a] in Him would receive; for the Holy[b] Spirit was not yet *given,* because Jesus was not yet glorified.

Who Is He?

[40]Therefore many[a] from the crowd, when they heard this saying, said, "Truly this is the Prophet." [41]Others said, "This is the Christ."

But some said, "Will the Christ come out of Galilee? [42]Has not the Scripture

---

7:33 [a]NU-Text and M-Text omit *to them.* 7:39 [a]NU-Text reads *who believed.* [b]NU-Text omits *Holy.* 7:40 [a]NU-Text reads *some.*

said that the Christ comes from the seed of David and from the town of Bethlehem, where David was?" 43So there was a division among the people because of Him. 44Now some of them wanted to take Him, but no one laid hands on Him.

Rejected by the Authorities

45Then the officers came to the chief priests and Pharisees, who said to them, "Why have you not brought Him?"

46The officers answered, "No man ever spoke like this Man!"

47Then the Pharisees answered them, "Are you also deceived? 48Have any of the rulers or the Pharisees believed in Him? 49But this crowd that does not know the law is accursed."

50Nicodemus (he who came to Jesus by night,a being one of them) said to them, 51"Does our law judge a man before it hears him and knows what he is doing?"

52They answered and said to him, "Are you also from Galilee? Search and look, for no prophet has arisena out of Galilee."

An Adulteress Faces the Light of the World

53And everyone went to his *own* house.a

7:50 aNU-Text reads *before*.   7:52 aNU-Text reads *is to rise*.   7:53 aThe words *And everyone* through *sin no more* (8:11) are bracketed by NU-Text as not original. They are present in over 900 manuscripts.

8 But Jesus went to the Mount of Olives.

2 Now early[a] in the morning He came again into the temple, and all the people came to Him; and He sat down and taught them. 3 Then the scribes and Pharisees brought to Him a woman caught in adultery. And when they had set her in the midst, 4 they said to Him, "Teacher, this woman was caught[a] in adultery, in the very act. 5 Now Moses, in the law, commanded[a] us that such should be stoned.[b] But what do You say?"[c] 6 This they said, testing Him, that they might have *something* of which to accuse Him. But Jesus stooped down and wrote on the ground with *His* finger, as though He did not hear.[a]

7 So when they continued asking Him, He raised Himself up[a] and said to them, "He who is without sin among you, let him throw a stone at her first." 8 And again He stooped down and wrote on the ground. 9 Then those who heard *it,* being convicted by *their* conscience,[a] went out one by one, beginning with the oldest *even* to the last. And Jesus was left alone, and the woman standing in the midst. 10 When Jesus had raised Himself up and saw no

8:2 [a]M-Text reads *very early.* 8:4 [a]M-Text reads *we found this woman.* 8:5 [a]M-Text reads *in our law Moses commanded.* [b]NU-Text and M-Text read *to stone such.* [c]M-Text adds *about her.* 8:6 [a]NU-Text and M-Text omit *as though He did not hear.* 8:7 [a]M-Text reads *He looked up.* 8:9 [a]NU-Text and M-Text omit *being convicted by their conscience.*

one but the woman, He said to her,[a]
"Woman, where are those accusers of
yours?[b] Has no one condemned you?"

[11]She said, "No one, Lord."

And Jesus said to her, "Neither do I
condemn you; go and[a] sin no more."

[12]Then Jesus spoke to them again,
saying, "I am the light of the world. He
who follows Me shall not walk in darkness, but have the light of life."

Jesus Defends His Self-Witness

[13]The Pharisees therefore said to
Him, "You bear witness of Yourself;
Your witness is not true."

[14]Jesus answered and said to them,
"Even if I bear witness of Myself, My
witness is true, for I know where I
came from and where I am going; but
you do not know where I come from
and where I am going. [15]You judge according to the flesh; I judge no one.
[16]And yet if I do judge, My judgment is
true; for I am not alone, but I *am* with
the Father who sent Me. [17]It is also
written in your law that the testimony
of two men is true. [18]I am One who
bears witness of Myself, and the Father
who sent Me bears witness of Me."

[19]Then they said to Him, "Where is
Your Father?"

Jesus answered, "You know neither
Me nor My Father. If you had known

8:10 [a]NU-Text omits *and saw no one but the woman;*
M-Text reads *He saw her and said.* [b]NU-Text and M-Text
omit *of yours.*   8:11 [a]NU-Text and M-Text add *from now
on.*

Me, you would have known My Father also."

²⁰These words Jesus spoke in the treasury, as He taught in the temple; and no one laid hands on Him, for His hour had not yet come.

Jesus Predicts His Departure

²¹Then Jesus said to them again, "I am going away, and you will seek Me, and will die in your sin. Where I go you cannot come."

²²So the Jews said, "Will He kill Himself, because He says, 'Where I go you cannot come'?"

²³And He said to them, "You are from beneath; I am from above. You are of this world; I am not of this world. ²⁴Therefore I said to you that you will die in your sins; for if you do not believe that I am *He,* you will die in your sins."

²⁵Then they said to Him, "Who are You?"

And Jesus said to them, "Just what I have been saying to you from the beginning. ²⁶I have many things to say and to judge concerning you, but He who sent Me is true; and I speak to the world those things which I heard from Him."

²⁷They did not understand that He spoke to them of the Father.

²⁸Then Jesus said to them, "When you lift up the Son of Man, then you will know that I am *He,* and *that* I do

nothing of Myself; but as My Father taught Me, I speak these things. [29]And He who sent Me is with Me. The Father has not left Me alone, for I always do those things that please Him." [30]As He spoke these words, many believed in Him.

The Truth Shall Make You Free

[31]Then Jesus said to those Jews who believed Him, "If you abide in My word, you are My disciples indeed. [32]And you shall know the truth, and the truth shall make you free."

[33]They answered Him, "We are Abraham's descendants, and have never been in bondage to anyone. How *can* You say, 'You will be made free'?"

[34]Jesus answered them, "Most assuredly, I say to you, whoever commits sin is a slave of sin. [35]And a slave does not abide in the house forever, *but* a son abides forever. [36]Therefore if the Son makes you free, you shall be free indeed.

Abraham's Seed and Satan's

[37]"I know that you are Abraham's descendants, but you seek to kill Me, because My word has no place in you. [38]I speak what I have seen with My Father, and you do what you have seen with[a] your father."

[39]They answered and said to Him, "Abraham is our father."

8:38 [a]NU-Text reads *heard from.*

Jesus said to them, "If you were Abraham's children, you would do the works of Abraham. [40]But now you seek to kill Me, a Man who has told you the truth which I heard from God. Abraham did not do this. [41]You do the deeds of your father."

Then they said to Him, "We were not born of fornication; we have one Father—God."

[42]Jesus said to them, "If God were your Father, you would love Me, for I proceeded forth and came from God; nor have I come of Myself, but He sent Me. [43]Why do you not understand My speech? Because you are not able to listen to My word. [44]You are of *your* father the devil, and the desires of your father you want to do. He was a murderer from the beginning, and does not stand in the truth, because there is no truth in him. When he speaks a lie, he speaks from his own *resources,* for he is a liar and the father of it. [45]But because I tell the truth, you do not believe Me. [46]Which of you convicts Me of sin? And if I tell the truth, why do you not believe Me? [47]He who is of God hears God's words; therefore you do not hear, because you are not of God."

Before Abraham Was, I AM

[48]Then the Jews answered and said to Him, "Do we not say rightly that You are a Samaritan and have a demon?"

[49]Jesus answered, "I do not have a

demon; but I honor My Father, and you dishonor Me. [50]And I do not seek My *own* glory; there is One who seeks and judges. [51]Most assuredly, I say to you, if anyone keeps My word he shall never see death."

[52]Then the Jews said to Him, "Now we know that You have a demon! Abraham is dead, and the prophets; and You say, 'If anyone keeps My word he shall never taste death.' [53]Are You greater than our father Abraham, who is dead? And the prophets are dead. Who do You make Yourself out to be?"

[54]Jesus answered, "If I honor Myself, My honor is nothing. It is My Father who honors Me, of whom you say that He is your[a] God. [55]Yet you have not known Him, but I know Him. And if I say, 'I do not know Him,' I shall be a liar like you; but I do know Him and keep His word. [56]Your father Abraham rejoiced to see My day, and he saw *it* and was glad."

[57]Then the Jews said to Him, "You are not yet fifty years old, and have You seen Abraham?"

[58]Jesus said to them, "Most assuredly, I say to you, before Abraham was, I AM."

[59]Then they took up stones to throw at Him; but Jesus hid Himself and went out of the temple,[a] going through the midst of them, and so passed by.

8:54 [a]NU-Text and M-Text read *our*. 8:59 [a]NU-Text omits the rest of this verse.

A Man Born Blind
Receives Sight

9 Now as *Jesus* passed by, He saw a man who was blind from birth. [2]And His disciples asked Him, saying, "Rabbi, who sinned, this man or his parents, that he was born blind?"

[3]Jesus answered, "Neither this man nor his parents sinned, but that the works of God should be revealed in him. [4]I[a] must work the works of Him who sent Me while it is day; *the* night is coming when no one can work. [5]As long as I am in the world, I am the light of the world."

[6]When He had said these things, He spat on the ground and made clay with the saliva; and He anointed the eyes of the blind man with the clay. [7]And He said to him, "Go, wash in the pool of Siloam" (which is translated, Sent). So he went and washed, and came back seeing.

[8]Therefore the neighbors and those who previously had seen that he was blind[a] said, "Is not this he who sat and begged?"

[9]Some said, "This is he." Others *said,* "He is like him."[a]

He said, "I am *he.*"

[10]Therefore they said to him, "How were your eyes opened?"

[11]He answered and said, "A Man called Jesus made clay and anointed my

9:4 [a]NU-Text reads *We.*   9:8 [a]NU-Text reads *a beggar.*
9:9 [a]NU-Text reads *"No, but he is like him."*

eyes and said to me, 'Go to the pool of[a] Siloam and wash.' So I went and washed, and I received sight."

¹²Then they said to him, "Where is He?"

He said, "I do not know."

The Pharisees Excommunicate the Healed Man

¹³They brought him who formerly was blind to the Pharisees. ¹⁴Now it was a Sabbath when Jesus made the clay and opened his eyes. ¹⁵Then the Pharisees also asked him again how he had received his sight. He said to them, "He put clay on my eyes, and I washed, and I see."

¹⁶Therefore some of the Pharisees said, "This Man is not from God, because He does not keep the Sabbath."

Others said, "How can a man who is a sinner do such signs?" And there was a division among them.

¹⁷They said to the blind man again, "What do you say about Him because He opened your eyes?"

He said, "He is a prophet."

¹⁸But the Jews did not believe concerning him, that he had been blind and received his sight, until they called the parents of him who had received his sight. ¹⁹And they asked them, saying, "Is this your son, who you say was born blind? How then does he now see?"

²⁰His parents answered them and said, "We know that this is our son,

---

9:11 ªNU-Text omits *the pool of.*

and that he was born blind; ²¹but by what means he now sees we do not know, or who opened his eyes we do not know. He is of age; ask him. He will speak for himself." ²²His parents said these *things* because they feared the Jews, for the Jews had agreed already that if anyone confessed *that* He *was* Christ, he would be put out of the synagogue. ²³Therefore his parents said, "He is of age; ask him."

²⁴So they again called the man who was blind, and said to him, "Give God the glory! We know that this Man is a sinner."

²⁵He answered and said, "Whether He is a sinner *or not* I do not know. One thing I know: that though I was blind, now I see."

²⁶Then they said to him again, "What did He do to you? How did He open your eyes?"

²⁷He answered them, "I told you already, and you did not listen. Why do you want to hear *it* again? Do you also want to become His disciples?"

²⁸Then they reviled him and said, "You are His disciple, but we are Moses' disciples. ²⁹We know that God spoke to Moses; *as for* this *fellow*, we do not know where He is from."

³⁰The man answered and said to them, "Why, this is a marvelous thing, that you do not know where He is from; yet He has opened my eyes! ³¹Now we know that God does not hear sinners;

but if anyone is a worshiper of God and does His will, He hears him. ³²Since the world began it has been unheard of that anyone opened the eyes of one who was born blind. ³³If this Man were not from God, He could do nothing."

³⁴They answered and said to him, "You were completely born in sins, and are you teaching us?" And they cast him out.

True Vision and True Blindness

³⁵Jesus heard that they had cast him out; and when He had found him, He said to him, "Do you believe in the Son of God?"^a

³⁶He answered and said, "Who is He, Lord, that I may believe in Him?"

³⁷And Jesus said to him, "You have both seen Him and it is He who is talking with you."

³⁸Then he said, "Lord, I believe!" And he worshiped Him.

³⁹And Jesus said, "For judgment I have come into this world, that those who do not see may see, and that those who see may be made blind."

⁴⁰Then *some* of the Pharisees who were with Him heard these words, and said to Him, "Are we blind also?"

⁴¹Jesus said to them, "If you were blind, you would have no sin; but now you say, 'We see.' Therefore your sin remains.

9:35 ^aNU-Text reads *Son of Man.*

Jesus the True Shepherd

10 "Most assuredly, I say to you, he who does not enter the sheepfold by the door, but climbs up some other way, the same is a thief and a robber. [2]But he who enters by the door is the shepherd of the sheep. [3]To him the doorkeeper opens, and the sheep hear his voice; and he calls his own sheep by name and leads them out. [4]And when he brings out his own sheep, he goes before them; and the sheep follow him, for they know his voice. [5]Yet they will by no means follow a stranger, but will flee from him, for they do not know the voice of strangers." [6]Jesus used this illustration, but they did not understand the things which He spoke to them.

Jesus the Good Shepherd

[7]Then Jesus said to them again, "Most assuredly, I say to you, I am the door of the sheep. [8]All who *ever* came before Me[a] are thieves and robbers, but the sheep did not hear them. [9]I am the door. If anyone enters by Me, he will be saved, and will go in and out and find pasture. [10]The thief does not come except to steal, and to kill, and to destroy. I have come that they may have life, and that they may have *it* more abundantly.

[11]"I am the good shepherd. The good shepherd gives His life for the

---

10:8 [a]M-Text omits *before Me*.

sheep. ¹²But a hireling, *he who is* not the shepherd, one who does not own the sheep, sees the wolf coming and leaves the sheep and flees; and the wolf catches the sheep and scatters them. ¹³The hireling flees because he is a hireling and does not care about the sheep. ¹⁴I am the good shepherd; and I know My *sheep,* and am known by My own. ¹⁵As the Father knows Me, even so I know the Father; and I lay down My life for the sheep. ¹⁶And other sheep I have which are not of this fold; them also I must bring, and they will hear My voice; and there will be one flock *and* one shepherd.

¹⁷"Therefore My Father loves Me, because I lay down My life that I may take it again. ¹⁸No one takes it from Me, but I lay it down of Myself. I have power to lay it down, and I have power to take it again. This command I have received from My Father."

¹⁹Therefore there was a division again among the Jews because of these sayings. ²⁰And many of them said, "He has a demon and is mad. Why do you listen to Him?"

²¹Others said, "These are not the words of one who has a demon. Can a demon open the eyes of the blind?"

The Shepherd Knows His Sheep

²²Now it was the Feast of Dedication in Jerusalem, and it was winter. ²³And Jesus walked in the temple, in Solomon's

porch. ²⁴Then the Jews surrounded Him and said to Him, "How long do You keep us in doubt? If You are the Christ, tell us plainly."

²⁵Jesus answered them, "I told you, and you do not believe. The works that I do in My Father's name, they bear witness of Me. ²⁶But you do not believe, because you are not of My sheep, as I said to you.ª ²⁷My sheep hear My voice, and I know them, and they follow Me. ²⁸And I give them eternal life, and they shall never perish; neither shall anyone snatch them out of My hand. ²⁹My Father, who has given *them* to Me, is greater than all; and no one is able to snatch *them* out of My Father's hand. ³⁰I and *My* Father are one."

Renewed Efforts to Stone Jesus

³¹Then the Jews took up stones again to stone Him. ³²Jesus answered them, "Many good works I have shown you from My Father. For which of those works do you stone Me?"

³³The Jews answered Him, saying, "For a good work we do not stone You, but for blasphemy, and because You, being a Man, make Yourself God."

³⁴Jesus answered them, "Is it not written in your law, *I said, "You are gods"* ?ª ³⁵If He called them gods, to whom the word of God came (and the Scripture cannot be broken), ³⁶do you say of Him whom the Father sanctified

10:26 ªNU-Text omits *as I said to you.*   10:34 ªPsalm 82:6

and sent into the world, 'You are blaspheming,' because I said, 'I am the Son of God'? [37]If I do not do the works of My Father, do not believe Me; [38]but if I do, though you do not believe Me, believe the works, that you may know and believe[a] that the Father *is* in Me, and I in Him." [39]Therefore they sought again to seize Him, but He escaped out of their hand.

The Believers Beyond Jordan

[40]And He went away again beyond the Jordan to the place where John was baptizing at first, and there He stayed. [41]Then many came to Him and said, "John performed no sign, but all the things that John spoke about this Man were true." [42]And many believed in Him there.

The Death of Lazarus

11 Now a certain *man* was sick, Lazarus of Bethany, the town of Mary and her sister Martha. [2]It was *that* Mary who anointed the Lord with fragrant oil and wiped His feet with her hair, whose brother Lazarus was sick. [3]Therefore the sisters sent to Him, saying, "Lord, behold, he whom You love is sick."

[4]When Jesus heard *that,* He said, "This sickness is not unto death, but for the glory of God, that the Son of God may be glorified through it."

10:38 [a]NU-Text reads *understand.*

⁵Now Jesus loved Martha and her sister and Lazarus. ⁶So, when He heard that he was sick, He stayed two more days in the place where He was. ⁷Then after this He said to *the* disciples, "Let us go to Judea again."

⁸*The* disciples said to Him, "Rabbi, lately the Jews sought to stone You, and are You going there again?"

⁹Jesus answered, "Are there not twelve hours in the day? If anyone walks in the day, he does not stumble, because he sees the light of this world. ¹⁰But if one walks in the night, he stumbles, because the light is not in him." ¹¹These things He said, and after that He said to them, "Our friend Lazarus sleeps, but I go that I may wake him up."

¹²Then His disciples said, "Lord, if he sleeps he will get well." ¹³However, Jesus spoke of his death, but they thought that He was speaking about taking rest in sleep.

¹⁴Then Jesus said to them plainly, "Lazarus is dead. ¹⁵And I am glad for your sakes that I was not there, that you may believe. Nevertheless let us go to him."

¹⁶Then Thomas, who is called the Twin, said to his fellow disciples, "Let us also go, that we may die with Him."

I Am the Resurrection and the Life

¹⁷So when Jesus came, He found that he had already been in the tomb four

days. ¹⁸Now Bethany was near Jerusalem, about two miles^a away. ¹⁹And many of the Jews had joined the women around Martha and Mary, to comfort them concerning their brother.

²⁰Now Martha, as soon as she heard that Jesus was coming, went and met Him, but Mary was sitting in the house. ²¹Now Martha said to Jesus, "Lord, if You had been here, my brother would not have died. ²²But even now I know that whatever You ask of God, God will give You."

²³Jesus said to her, "Your brother will rise again."

²⁴Martha said to Him, "I know that he will rise again in the resurrection at the last day."

²⁵Jesus said to her, "I am the resurrection and the life. He who believes in Me, though he may die, he shall live. ²⁶And whoever lives and believes in Me shall never die. Do you believe this?"

²⁷She said to Him, "Yes, Lord, I believe that You are the Christ, the Son of God, who is to come into the world."

Jesus and Death, the Last Enemy

²⁸And when she had said these things, she went her way and secretly called Mary her sister, saying, "The Teacher has come and is calling for you." ²⁹As soon as she heard *that,* she arose quickly and came to Him. ³⁰Now

---

11:18 ^aLiterally *fifteen stadia*

Jesus had not yet come into the town, but was[a] in the place where Martha met Him. ³¹Then the Jews who were with her in the house, and comforting her, when they saw that Mary rose up quickly and went out, followed her, saying, "She is going to the tomb to weep there."[a]

³²Then, when Mary came where Jesus was, and saw Him, she fell down at His feet, saying to Him, "Lord, if You had been here, my brother would not have died."

³³Therefore, when Jesus saw her weeping, and the Jews who came with her weeping, He groaned in the spirit and was troubled. ³⁴And He said, "Where have you laid him?"

They said to Him, "Lord, come and see."

³⁵Jesus wept. ³⁶Then the Jews said, "See how He loved him!"

³⁷And some of them said, "Could not this Man, who opened the eyes of the blind, also have kept this man from dying?"

Lazarus Raised from the Dead

³⁸Then Jesus, again groaning in Himself, came to the tomb. It was a cave, and a stone lay against it. ³⁹Jesus said, "Take away the stone."

Martha, the sister of him who was dead, said to Him, "Lord, by this time there is a stench, for he has been *dead*

11:30 [a]NU-Text adds *still.*   11:31 [a]NU-Text reads *supposing that she was going to the tomb to weep there.*

four days."

⁴⁰Jesus said to her, "Did I not say to you that if you would believe you would see the glory of God?" ⁴¹Then they took away the stone *from the place* where the dead man was lying.ᵃ And Jesus lifted up *His* eyes and said, "Father, I thank You that You have heard Me. ⁴²And I know that You always hear Me, but because of the people who are standing by I said *this,* that they may believe that You sent Me." ⁴³Now when He had said these things, He cried with a loud voice, "Lazarus, come forth!" ⁴⁴And he who had died came out bound hand and foot with graveclothes, and his face was wrapped with a cloth. Jesus said to them, "Loose him, and let him go."

The Plot to Kill Jesus

⁴⁵Then many of the Jews who had come to Mary, and had seen the things Jesus did, believed in Him. ⁴⁶But some of them went away to the Pharisees and told them the things Jesus did. ⁴⁷Then the chief priests and the Pharisees gathered a council and said, "What shall we do? For this Man works many signs. ⁴⁸If we let Him alone like this, everyone will believe in Him, and the Romans will come and take away both our place and nation."

⁴⁹And one of them, Caiaphas, being high priest that year, said to them, "You

---

11:41 ᵃNU-Text omits *from the place where the dead man was lying.*

know nothing at all, [50]nor do you consider that it is expedient for us[a] that one man should die for the people, and not that the whole nation should perish." [51]Now this he did not say on his own *authority;* but being high priest that year he prophesied that Jesus would die for the nation, [52]and not for that nation only, but also that He would gather together in one the children of God who were scattered abroad.

[53]Then, from that day on, they plotted to put Him to death. [54]Therefore Jesus no longer walked openly among the Jews, but went from there into the country near the wilderness, to a city called Ephraim, and there remained with His disciples.

[55]And the Passover of the Jews was near, and many went from the country up to Jerusalem before the Passover, to purify themselves. [56]Then they sought Jesus, and spoke among themselves as they stood in the temple, "What do you think—that He will not come to the feast?" [57]Now both the chief priests and the Pharisees had given a command, that if anyone knew where He was, he should report *it,* that they might seize Him.

The Anointing at Bethany

12 Then, six days before the Passover, Jesus came to Bethany, where Lazarus was who had been dead,[a] whom He had raised from the

---

11:50 [a]NU-Text reads *you.*   12:1 [a]NU-Text omits *who had been dead.*

dead. [2]There they made Him a supper; and Martha served, but Lazarus was one of those who sat at the table with Him. [3]Then Mary took a pound of very costly oil of spikenard, anointed the feet of Jesus, and wiped His feet with her hair. And the house was filled with the fragrance of the oil.

[4]But one of His disciples, Judas Iscariot, Simon's *son,* who would betray Him, said, [5]"Why was this fragrant oil not sold for three hundred denarii[a] and given to the poor?" [6]This he said, not that he cared for the poor, but because he was a thief, and had the money box; and he used to take what was put in it.

[7]But Jesus said, "Let her alone; she has kept[a] this for the day of My burial. [8]For the poor you have with you always, but Me you do not have always."

The Plot to Kill Lazarus

[9]Now a great many of the Jews knew that He was there; and they came, not for Jesus' sake only, but that they might also see Lazarus, whom He had raised from the dead. [10]But the chief priests plotted to put Lazarus to death also, [11]because on account of him many of the Jews went away and believed in Jesus.

The Triumphal Entry

[12]The next day a great multitude that had come to the feast, when they

12:5 [a]About one year's wages for a worker   12:7 [a]NU-Text reads *that she may keep.*

heard that Jesus was coming to Jerusalem, [13]took branches of palm trees and went out to meet Him, and cried out:

"Hosanna!
'Blessed is He who comes in the
        name of the LORD!'[a]
The King of Israel!"

[14]Then Jesus, when He had found a young donkey, sat on it; as it is written:

[15]"Fear not, daughter of Zion;
Behold, your King is coming,
Sitting on a donkey's colt."[a]

[16]His disciples did not understand these things at first; but when Jesus was glorified, then they remembered that these things were written about Him and *that* they had done these things to Him.

[17]Therefore the people, who were with Him when He called Lazarus out of his tomb and raised him from the dead, bore witness. [18]For this reason the people also met Him, because they heard that He had done this sign. [19]The Pharisees therefore said among themselves, "You see that you are accomplishing nothing. Look, the world has gone after Him!"

The Fruitful Grain of Wheat

[20]Now there were certain Greeks among those who came up to worship

12:13 [a]Psalm 118:26   12:15 [a]Zechariah 9:9

at the feast. [21]Then they came to Philip, who was from Bethsaida of Galilee, and asked him, saying, "Sir, we wish to see Jesus."

[22]Philip came and told Andrew, and in turn Andrew and Philip told Jesus.

[23]But Jesus answered them, saying, "The hour has come that the Son of Man should be glorified. [24]Most assuredly, I say to you, unless a grain of wheat falls into the ground and dies, it remains alone; but if it dies, it produces much grain. [25]He who loves his life will lose it, and he who hates his life in this world will keep it for eternal life. [26]If anyone serves Me, let him follow Me; and where I am, there My servant will be also. If anyone serves Me, him *My* Father will honor.

Jesus Predicts His Death on the Cross

[27]"Now My soul is troubled, and what shall I say? 'Father, save Me from this hour'? But for this purpose I came to this hour. [28]Father, glorify Your name."

Then a voice came from heaven, *saying,* "I have both glorified *it* and will glorify *it* again."

[29]Therefore the people who stood by and heard *it* said that it had thundered. Others said, "An angel has spoken to Him."

[30]Jesus answered and said, "This voice did not come because of Me, but

for your sake. [31]Now is the judgment of this world; now the ruler of this world will be cast out. [32]And I, if I am lifted up from the earth, will draw all *peoples* to Myself." [33]This He said, signifying by what death He would die.

[34]The people answered Him, "We have heard from the law that the Christ remains forever; and how *can* You say, 'The Son of Man must be lifted up'? Who is this Son of Man?"

[35]Then Jesus said to them, "A little while longer the light is with you. Walk while you have the light, lest darkness overtake you; he who walks in darkness does not know where he is going. [36]While you have the light, believe in the light, that you may become sons of light." These things Jesus spoke, and departed, and was hidden from them.

Who Has Believed Our Report?

[37]But although He had done so many signs before them, they did not believe in Him, [38]that the word of Isaiah the prophet might be fulfilled, which he spoke:

> "Lord, who has believed our report?
> And to whom has the arm of the
>   LORD been revealed?"[a]

[39]Therefore they could not believe, because Isaiah said again:

12:38 [a]Isaiah 53:1

^{40}*"He has blinded their eyes and
      hardened their hearts,
Lest they should see with their eyes,
Lest they should understand with
      their hearts and turn,
So that I should heal them."*[a]

^{41}These things Isaiah said when[a] he saw His glory and spoke of Him.

Walk in the Light

^{42}Nevertheless even among the rulers many believed in Him, but because of the Pharisees they did not confess Him, lest they should be put out of the synagogue; ^{43}for they loved the praise of men more than the praise of God.

^{44}Then Jesus cried out and said, "He who believes in Me, believes not in Me but in Him who sent Me. ^{45}And he who sees Me sees Him who sent Me. ^{46}I have come *as* a light into the world, that whoever believes in Me should not abide in darkness. ^{47}And if anyone hears My words and does not believe,[a] I do not judge him; for I did not come to judge the world but to save the world. ^{48}He who rejects Me, and does not receive My words, has that which judges him—the word that I have spoken will judge him in the last day. ^{49}For I have not spoken on My own *authority*; but the Father who sent Me gave Me a command, what I should say and what

12:40 [a]Isaiah 6:10   12:41 [a]NU-Text reads *because*. 12:47 [a]NU-Text reads *keep them*.

I should speak. ⁵⁰And I know that His command is everlasting life. Therefore, whatever I speak, just as the Father has told Me, so I speak."

Jesus Washes the Disciples' Feet

13 Now before the Feast of the Passover, when Jesus knew that His hour had come that He should depart from this world to the Father, having loved His own who were in the world, He loved them to the end.

²And supper being ended,ᵃ the devil having already put it into the heart of Judas Iscariot, Simon's *son,* to betray Him, ³Jesus, knowing that the Father had given all things into His hands, and that He had come from God and was going to God, ⁴rose from supper and laid aside His garments, took a towel and girded Himself. ⁵After that, He poured water into a basin and began to wash the disciples' feet, and to wipe *them* with the towel with which He was girded. ⁶Then He came to Simon Peter. And *Peter* said to Him, "Lord, are You washing my feet?"

⁷Jesus answered and said to him, "What I am doing you do not understand now, but you will know after this."

⁸Peter said to Him, "You shall never wash my feet!"

Jesus answered him, "If I do not

13:2 ᵃNU-Text reads *And during supper.*

wash you, you have no part with Me."

⁹Simon Peter said to Him, "Lord, not my feet only, but also *my* hands and *my* head!"

¹⁰Jesus said to him, "He who is bathed needs only to wash *his* feet, but is completely clean; and you are clean, but not all of you." ¹¹For He knew who would betray Him; therefore He said, "You are not all clean."

¹²So when He had washed their feet, taken His garments, and sat down again, He said to them, "Do you know what I have done to you? ¹³You call Me Teacher and Lord, and you say well, for *so* I am. ¹⁴If I then, *your* Lord and Teacher, have washed your feet, you also ought to wash one another's feet. ¹⁵For I have given you an example, that you should do as I have done to you. ¹⁶Most assuredly, I say to you, a servant is not greater than his master; nor is he who is sent greater than he who sent him. ¹⁷If you know these things, blessed are you if you do them.

Jesus Identifies His Betrayer

¹⁸"I do not speak concerning all of you. I know whom I have chosen; but that the Scripture may be fulfilled, *'He who eats bread with Me*ᵃ *has lifted up his heel against Me.'*ᵇ ¹⁹Now I tell you before it comes, that when it does come to pass, you may believe that I am *He.* ²⁰Most assuredly, I say to you, he who

---

13:18 ᵃNU-Text reads *My bread.* ᵇPsalm 41:9

receives whomever I send receives Me; and he who receives Me receives Him who sent Me."

²¹When Jesus had said these things, He was troubled in spirit, and testified and said, "Most assuredly, I say to you, one of you will betray Me." ²²Then the disciples looked at one another, perplexed about whom He spoke.

²³Now there was leaning on Jesus' bosom one of His disciples, whom Jesus loved. ²⁴Simon Peter therefore motioned to him to ask who it was of whom He spoke.

²⁵Then, leaning back[a] on Jesus' breast, he said to Him, "Lord, who is it?"

²⁶Jesus answered, "It is he to whom I shall give a piece of bread when I have dipped *it*." And having dipped the bread, He gave *it* to Judas Iscariot, *the son* of Simon. ²⁷Now after the piece of bread, Satan entered him. Then Jesus said to him, "What you do, do quickly." ²⁸But no one at the table knew for what reason He said this to him. ²⁹For some thought, because Judas had the money box, that Jesus had said to him, "Buy *those things* we need for the feast," or that he should give something to the poor.

³⁰Having received the piece of bread, he then went out immediately. And it was night.

13:25 [a]NU-Text and M-Text add *thus*.

The New Commandment

[31]So, when he had gone out, Jesus said, "Now the Son of Man is glorified, and God is glorified in Him. [32]If God is glorified in Him, God will also glorify Him in Himself, and glorify Him immediately. [33]Little children, I shall be with you a little while longer. You will seek Me; and as I said to the Jews, 'Where I am going, you cannot come,' so now I say to you. [34]A new commandment I give to you, that you love one another; as I have loved you, that you also love one another. [35]By this all will know that you are My disciples, if you have love for one another."

Jesus Predicts Peter's Denial

[36]Simon Peter said to Him, "Lord, where are You going?"

Jesus answered him, "Where I am going you cannot follow Me now, but you shall follow Me afterward."

[37]Peter said to Him, "Lord, why can I not follow You now? I will lay down my life for Your sake."

[38]Jesus answered him, "Will you lay down your life for My sake? Most assuredly, I say to you, the rooster shall not crow till you have denied Me three times.

The Way, the Truth, and the Life

14 "Let not your heart be troubled; you believe in God, believe also in Me. ²In My Father's house are many mansions;ᵃ if *it were* not *so,* I would have told you. I go to prepare a place for you.ᵇ ³And if I go and prepare a place for you, I will come again and receive you to Myself; that where I am, *there* you may be also. ⁴And where I go you know, and the way you know."

⁵Thomas said to Him, "Lord, we do not know where You are going, and how can we know the way?" ⁶Jesus said to him, "I am the way, the truth, and the life. No one comes to the Father except through Me.

The Father Revealed

⁷"If you had known Me, you would have known My Father also; and from now on you know Him and have seen Him."

⁸Philip said to Him, "Lord, show us the Father, and it is sufficient for us."

⁹Jesus said to him, "Have I been with you so long, and yet you have not known Me, Philip? He who has seen Me has seen the Father; so how can you say, 'Show us the Father'? ¹⁰Do you not believe that I am in the Father, and the Father in Me? The words that I speak to you I do not speak on My own *authority;* but the Father who dwells in Me does the works. ¹¹Believe Me that I *am* in the Father and the Father in Me,

14:2 ᵃLiterally *dwellings* ᵇNU-Text adds a word which would cause the text to read either *if it were not so, would I have told you that I go to prepare a place for you?* or *if it were not so I would have told you; for I go to prepare a place for you.*

or else believe Me for the sake of the works themselves.

The Answered Prayer

¹²"Most assuredly, I say to you, he who believes in Me, the works that I do he will do also; and greater *works* than these he will do, because I go to My Father. ¹³And whatever you ask in My name, that I will do, that the Father may be glorified in the Son. ¹⁴If you ask[a] anything in My name, I will do *it*.

Jesus Promises Another Helper

¹⁵"If you love Me, keep[a] My commandments. ¹⁶And I will pray the Father, and He will give you another Helper, that He may abide with you forever— ¹⁷the Spirit of truth, whom the world cannot receive, because it neither sees Him nor knows Him; but you know Him, for He dwells with you and will be in you. ¹⁸I will not leave you orphans; I will come to you.

Indwelling of the Father and the Son

¹⁹"A little while longer and the world will see Me no more, but you will see Me. Because I live, you will live also. ²⁰At that day you will know that I *am* in My Father, and you in Me, and I in you. ²¹He who has My commandments and keeps them, it is he who loves Me. And he who loves Me will be

---

14:14 ªNU-Text adds *Me*.   14:15 ªNU-Text reads *you will keep*.

loved by My Father, and I will love him and manifest Myself to him."

²²Judas (not Iscariot) said to Him, "Lord, how is it that You will manifest Yourself to us, and not to the world?"

²³Jesus answered and said to him, "If anyone loves Me, he will keep My word; and My Father will love him, and We will come to him and make Our home with him. ²⁴He who does not love Me does not keep My words; and the word which you hear is not Mine but the Father's who sent Me.

The Gift of His Peace

²⁵"These things I have spoken to you while being present with you. ²⁶But the Helper, the Holy Spirit, whom the Father will send in My name, He will teach you all things, and bring to your remembrance all things that I said to you. ²⁷Peace I leave with you, My peace I give to you; not as the world gives do I give to you. Let not your heart be troubled, neither let it be afraid. ²⁸You have heard Me say to you, 'I am going away and coming *back* to you.' If you loved Me, you would rejoice because I said,[a] 'I am going to the Father,' for My Father is greater than I.

²⁹"And now I have told you before it comes, that when it does come to pass, you may believe. ³⁰I will no longer talk much with you, for the ruler of this world is coming, and he

---

14:28 [a]NU-Text omits *I said*.

has nothing in Me. ³¹But that the world may know that I love the Father, and as the Father gave Me commandment, so I do. Arise, let us go from here.

The True Vine

15 "I am the true vine, and My Father is the vinedresser. ²Every branch in Me that does not bear fruit He takes away;ᵃ and every *branch* that bears fruit He prunes, that it may bear more fruit. ³You are already clean because of the word which I have spoken to you. ⁴Abide in Me, and I in you. As the branch cannot bear fruit of itself, unless it abides in the vine, neither can you, unless you abide in Me.

⁵"I am the vine, you *are* the branches. He who abides in Me, and I in him, bears much fruit; for without Me you can do nothing. ⁶If anyone does not abide in Me, he is cast out as a branch and is withered; and they gather them and throw *them* into the fire, and they are burned. ⁷If you abide in Me, and My words abide in you, you willᵃ ask what you desire, and it shall be done for you. ⁸By this My Father is glorified, that you bear much fruit; so you will be My disciples.

Love and Joy Perfected

⁹"As the Father loved Me, I also have loved you; abide in My love. ¹⁰If you keep My commandments, you will

---

15:2 ᵃOr *lifts up*   15:7 ᵃNU-Text omits *you will.*

abide in My love, just as I have kept My Father's commandments and abide in His love.

¹¹"These things I have spoken to you, that My joy may remain in you, and *that* your joy may be full. ¹²This is My commandment, that you love one another as I have loved you. ¹³Greater love has no one than this, than to lay down one's life for his friends. ¹⁴You are My friends if you do whatever I command you. ¹⁵No longer do I call you servants, for a servant does not know what his master is doing; but I have called you friends, for all things that I heard from My Father I have made known to you. ¹⁶You did not choose Me, but I chose you and appointed you that you should go and bear fruit, and *that* your fruit should remain, that whatever you ask the Father in My name He may give you. ¹⁷These things I command you, that you love one another.

The World's Hatred

¹⁸"If the world hates you, you know that it hated Me before *it hated* you. ¹⁹If you were of the world, the world would love its own. Yet because you are not of the world, but I chose you out of the world, therefore the world hates you. ²⁰Remember the word that I said to you, 'A servant is not greater than his master.' If they persecuted Me, they will also persecute you. If they kept My word, they will keep yours

also. [21]But all these things they will do to you for My name's sake, because they do not know Him who sent Me. [22]If I had not come and spoken to them, they would have no sin, but now they have no excuse for their sin. [23]He who hates Me hates My Father also. [24]If I had not done among them the works which no one else did, they would have no sin; but now they have seen and also hated both Me and My Father. [25]But *this happened* that the word might be fulfilled which is written in their law, *'They hated Me without a cause.'*[a]

The Coming Rejection

[26]"But when the Helper comes, whom I shall send to you from the Father, the Spirit of truth who proceeds from the Father, He will testify of Me. [27]And you also will bear witness, because you have been with Me from the beginning.

16
"These things I have spoken to you, that you should not be made to stumble. [2]They will put you out of the synagogues; yes, the time is coming that whoever kills you will think that he offers God service. [3]And these things they will do to you[a] because they have not known the Father nor Me. [4]But these things I have told you, that when the[a] time comes, you

---

15:25 [a]Psalm 69:4   16:3 [a]NU-Text and M-Text omit *to you.*   16:4 [a]NU-Text reads *their.*

may remember that I told you of them.

"And these things I did not say to you at the beginning, because I was with you.

The Work of the Holy Spirit

[5]"But now I go away to Him who sent Me, and none of you asks Me, 'Where are You going?' [6]But because I have said these things to you, sorrow has filled your heart. [7]Nevertheless I tell you the truth. It is to your advantage that I go away; for if I do not go away, the Helper will not come to you; but if I depart, I will send Him to you. [8]And when He has come, He will convict the world of sin, and of righteousness, and of judgment: [9]of sin, because they do not believe in Me; [10]of righteousness, because I go to My Father and you see Me no more; [11]of judgment, because the ruler of this world is judged.

[12]"I still have many things to say to you, but you cannot bear *them* now. [13]However, when He, the Spirit of truth, has come, He will guide you into all truth; for He will not speak on His own *authority,* but whatever He hears He will speak; and He will tell you things to come. [14]He will glorify Me, for He will take of what is Mine and declare *it* to you. [15]All things that the Father has are Mine. Therefore I said that He will take of Mine and declare *it* to you.[a]

16:15 [a]NU-Text and M-Text read *He takes of Mine and will declare it to you.*

Sorrow Will Turn to Joy

[16]"A little while, and you will not see Me; and again a little while, and you will see Me, because I go to the Father."

[17]Then *some* of His disciples said among themselves, "What is this that He says to us, 'A little while, and you will not see Me; and again a little while, and you will see Me'; and, 'because I go to the Father'?" [18]They said therefore, "What is this that He says, 'A little while'? We do not know what He is saying."

[19]Now Jesus knew that they desired to ask Him, and He said to them, "Are you inquiring among yourselves about what I said, 'A little while, and you will not see Me; and again a little while, and you will see Me'? [20]Most assuredly, I say to you that you will weep and lament, but the world will rejoice; and you will be sorrowful, but your sorrow will be turned into joy. [21]A woman, when she is in labor, has sorrow because her hour has come; but as soon as she has given birth to the child, she no longer remembers the anguish, for joy that a human being has been born into the world. [22]Therefore you now have sorrow; but I will see you again and your heart will rejoice, and your joy no one will take from you.

[23]"And in that day you will ask Me nothing. Most assuredly, I say to you, whatever you ask the Father in My name He will give you. [24]Until now you have asked nothing in My name.

Ask, and you will receive, that your joy
may be full.

Jesus Christ Has
Overcome the World

[25]"These things I have spoken to
you in figurative language; but the time
is coming when I will no longer speak
to you in figurative language, but I will
tell you plainly about the Father. [26]In
that day you will ask in My name, and
I do not say to you that I shall pray the
Father for you; [27]for the Father Himself
loves you, because you have loved Me,
and have believed that I came forth
from God. [28]I came forth from the Father and have come into the world.
Again, I leave the world and go to the
Father."

[29]His disciples said to Him, "See,
now You are speaking plainly, and using no figure of speech! [30]Now we are
sure that You know all things, and have
no need that anyone should question
You. By this we believe that You came
forth from God."

[31]Jesus answered them, "Do you
now believe? [32]Indeed the hour is coming, yes, has now come, that you will
be scattered, each to his own, and will
leave Me alone. And yet I am not alone,
because the Father is with Me. [33]These
things I have spoken to you, that in Me
you may have peace. In the world you
will[a] have tribulation; but be of good

16:33 [a]NU-Text and M-Text omit will.

cheer, I have overcome the world."

Jesus Prays for Himself

17 Jesus spoke these words, lifted up His eyes to heaven, and said: "Father, the hour has come. Glorify Your Son, that Your Son also may glorify You, ²as You have given Him authority over all flesh, that He should[a] give eternal life to as many as You have given Him. ³And this is eternal life, that they may know You, the only true God, and Jesus Christ whom You have sent. ⁴I have glorified You on the earth. I have finished the work which You have given Me to do. ⁵And now, O Father, glorify Me together with Yourself, with the glory which I had with You before the world was.

Jesus Prays for His Disciples

⁶"I have manifested Your name to the men whom You have given Me out of the world. They were Yours, You gave them to Me, and they have kept Your word. ⁷Now they have known that all things which You have given Me are from You. ⁸For I have given to them the words which You have given Me; and they have received *them,* and have known surely that I came forth from You; and they have believed that You sent Me.

⁹"I pray for them. I do not pray for the world but for those whom You

---

17:2 ªM-Text reads *shall.*

have given Me, for they are Yours.
[10]And all Mine are Yours, and Yours
are Mine, and I am glorified in them.
[11]Now I am no longer in the world, but
these are in the world, and I come to
You. Holy Father, keep through Your
name those whom You have given Me,[a]
that they may be one as We *are*.
[12]While I was with them in the world,[a]
I kept them in Your name. Those
whom You gave Me I have kept;[b] and
none of them is lost except the son of
perdition, that the Scripture might be
fulfilled. [13]But now I come to You, and
these things I speak in the world, that
they may have My joy fulfilled in themselves. [14]I have given them Your word;
and the world has hated them because
they are not of the world, just as I am
not of the world. [15]I do not pray that
You should take them out of the world,
but that You should keep them from
the evil one. [16]They are not of the
world, just as I am not of the world.
[17]Sanctify them by Your truth. Your
word is truth. [18]As You sent Me into
the world, I also have sent them into
the world. [19]And for their sakes I sanc-
tify Myself, that they also may be sanctified by the truth.

Jesus Prays for All Believers

[20]"I do not pray for these alone, but

17:11 [a]NU-Text and M-Text read *keep them through Your
name which You have given Me.* 17:12 [a]NU-Text omits *in
the world.* [b]NU-Text reads *in Your name which You gave
Me. And I guarded them;* (or *it;*).

also for those who will[a] believe in Me through their word; ²¹that they all may be one, as You, Father, *are* in Me, and I in You; that they also may be one in Us, that the world may believe that You sent Me. ²²And the glory which You gave Me I have given them, that they may be one just as We are one: ²³I in them, and You in Me; that they may be made perfect in one, and that the world may know that You have sent Me, and have loved them as You have loved Me.

²⁴"Father, I desire that they also whom You gave Me may be with Me where I am, that they may behold My glory which You have given Me; for You loved Me before the foundation of the world. ²⁵O righteous Father! The world has not known You, but I have known You; and these have known that You sent Me. ²⁶And I have declared to them Your name, and will declare *it,* that the love with which You loved Me may be in them, and I in them."

Betrayal and Arrest in Gethsemane

18 When Jesus had spoken these words, He went out with His disciples over the Brook Kidron, where there was a garden, which He and His disciples entered. ²And Judas, who betrayed Him, also knew the place; for Jesus often met there with His disciples. ³Then Judas, having received a detach-

---

17:20 [a]NU-Text and M-Text omit *will.*

ment *of troops,* and officers from the chief priests and Pharisees, came there with lanterns, torches, and weapons. [4]Jesus therefore, knowing all things that would come upon Him, went forward and said to them, "Whom are you seeking?"

[5]They answered Him, "Jesus of Nazareth."

Jesus said to them, "I am *He.*" And Judas, who betrayed Him, also stood with them. [6]Now when He said to them, "I am *He,*" they drew back and fell to the ground.

[7]Then He asked them again, "Whom are you seeking?"

And they said, "Jesus of Nazareth."

[8]Jesus answered, "I have told you that I am *He.* Therefore, if you seek Me, let these go their way," [9]that the saying might be fulfilled which He spoke, "Of those whom You gave Me I have lost none."

[10]Then Simon Peter, having a sword, drew it and struck the high priest's servant, and cut off his right ear. The servant's name was Malchus.

[11]So Jesus said to Peter, "Put your sword into the sheath. Shall I not drink the cup which My Father has given Me?"

Before the High Priest

[12]Then the detachment *of troops* and the captain and the officers of the Jews arrested Jesus and bound Him. [13]And they led Him away to Annas

first, for he was the father-in-law of
Caiaphas who was high priest that year.
¹⁴Now it was Caiaphas who advised
the Jews that it was expedient that one
man should die for the people.

Peter Denies Jesus

¹⁵And Simon Peter followed Jesus,
and so *did* another[a] disciple. Now that
disciple was known to the high priest,
and went with Jesus into the courtyard
of the high priest. ¹⁶But Peter stood at
the door outside. Then the other disciple, who was known to the high priest,
went out and spoke to her who kept
the door, and brought Peter in. ¹⁷Then
the servant girl who kept the door said
to Peter, "You are not also *one* of this
Man's disciples, are you?"

He said, "I am not."

¹⁸Now the servants and officers who
had made a fire of coals stood there, for
it was cold, and they warmed themselves. And Peter stood with them and
warmed himself.

Jesus Questioned by
the High Priest

¹⁹The high priest then asked Jesus
about His disciples and His doctrine.
²⁰Jesus answered him, "I spoke
openly to the world. I always taught in
synagogues and in the temple, where
the Jews always meet,[a] and in secret I
have said nothing. ²¹Why do you ask

18:15 ªM-Text reads *the other.*   18:20 ªNU-Text reads
where all the Jews meet.

Me? Ask those who have heard Me what I said to them. Indeed they know what I said."

[22]And when He had said these things, one of the officers who stood by struck Jesus with the palm of his hand, saying, "Do You answer the high priest like that?"

[23]Jesus answered him, "If I have spoken evil, bear witness of the evil; but if well, why do you strike Me?"

[24]Then Annas sent Him bound to Caiaphas the high priest.

Peter Denies Twice More

[25]Now Simon Peter stood and warmed himself. Therefore they said to him, "You are not also *one* of His disciples, are you?"

He denied *it* and said, "I am not!"

[26]One of the servants of the high priest, a relative *of him* whose ear Peter cut off, said, "Did I not see you in the garden with Him?" [27]Peter then denied again; and immediately a rooster crowed.

In Pilate's Court

[28]Then they led Jesus from Caiaphas to the Praetorium, and it was early morning. But they themselves did not go into the Praetorium, lest they should be defiled, but that they might eat the Passover. [29]Pilate then went out to them and said, "What accusation do you bring against this Man?"

[30]They answered and said to him, "If He were not an evildoer, we would

not have delivered Him up to you."

³¹Then Pilate said to them, "You take Him and judge Him according to your law."

Therefore the Jews said to him, "It is not lawful for us to put anyone to death," ³²that the saying of Jesus might be fulfilled which He spoke, signifying by what death He would die.

³³Then Pilate entered the Praetorium again, called Jesus, and said to Him, "Are You the King of the Jews?"

³⁴Jesus answered him, "Are you speaking for yourself about this, or did others tell you this concerning Me?"

³⁵Pilate answered, "Am I a Jew? Your own nation and the chief priests have delivered You to me. What have You done?"

³⁶Jesus answered, "My kingdom is not of this world. If My kingdom were of this world, My servants would fight, so that I should not be delivered to the Jews; but now My kingdom is not from here."

³⁷Pilate therefore said to Him, "Are You a king then?"

Jesus answered, "You say *rightly* that I am a king. For this cause I was born, and for this cause I have come into the world, that I should bear witness to the truth. Everyone who is of the truth hears My voice."

³⁸Pilate said to Him, "What is truth?" And when he had said this, he went out again to the Jews, and said to them, "I find no fault in Him at all.

Taking the Place of Barabbas

³⁹"But you have a custom that I should release someone to you at the Passover. Do you therefore want me to release to you the King of the Jews?"

⁴⁰Then they all cried again, saying, "Not this Man, but Barabbas!" Now Barabbas was a robber.

The Soldiers Mock Jesus

19 So then Pilate took Jesus and scourged *Him.* ²And the soldiers twisted a crown of thorns and put *it* on His head, and they put on Him a purple robe. ³Then they said,ᵃ "Hail, King of the Jews!" And they struck Him with their hands.

⁴Pilate then went out again, and said to them, "Behold, I am bringing Him out to you, that you may know that I find no fault in Him."

Pilate's Decision

⁵Then Jesus came out, wearing the crown of thorns and the purple robe. And *Pilate* said to them, "Behold the Man!"

⁶Therefore, when the chief priests and officers saw Him, they cried out, saying, "Crucify *Him,* crucify *Him!* "

Pilate said to them, "You take Him and crucify *Him,* for I find no fault in Him."

⁷The Jews answered him, "We have a law, and according to ourᵃ law He

19:3 ᵃNU-Text reads *And they came up to Him and said.*
19:7 ᵃNU-Text reads *the law.*

ought to die, because He made Himself the Son of God."

⁸Therefore, when Pilate heard that saying, he was the more afraid, ⁹and went again into the Praetorium, and said to Jesus, "Where are You from?" But Jesus gave him no answer.

¹⁰Then Pilate said to Him, "Are You not speaking to me? Do You not know that I have power to crucify You, and power to release You?"

¹¹Jesus answered, "You could have no power at all against Me unless it had been given you from above. Therefore the one who delivered Me to you has the greater sin."

¹²From then on Pilate sought to release Him, but the Jews cried out, saying, "If you let this Man go, you are not Caesar's friend. Whoever makes himself a king speaks against Caesar."

¹³When Pilate therefore heard that saying, he brought Jesus out and sat down in the judgment seat in a place that is called *The* Pavement, but in Hebrew, Gabbatha. ¹⁴Now it was the Preparation Day of the Passover, and about the sixth hour. And he said to the Jews, "Behold your King!"

¹⁵But they cried out, "Away with *Him,* away with *Him!* Crucify Him!"

Pilate said to them, "Shall I crucify your King?"

The chief priests answered, "We have no king but Caesar!"

¹⁶Then he delivered Him to them to

be crucified. Then they took Jesus and led *Him* away.[a]

The King on a Cross

[17]And He, bearing His cross, went out to a place called *the Place* of a Skull, which is called in Hebrew, Golgotha, [18]where they crucified Him, and two others with Him, one on either side, and Jesus in the center. [19]Now Pilate wrote a title and put *it* on the cross. And the writing was:

JESUS OF NAZARETH,
THE KING OF THE JEWS.

[20]Then many of the Jews read this title, for the place where Jesus was crucified was near the city; and it was written in Hebrew, Greek, *and* Latin.

[21]Therefore the chief priests of the Jews said to Pilate, "Do not write, 'The King of the Jews,' but, 'He said, "I am the King of the Jews." ' "

[22]Pilate answered, "What I have written, I have written."

[23]Then the soldiers, when they had crucified Jesus, took His garments and made four parts, to each soldier a part, and also the tunic. Now the tunic was without seam, woven from the top in one piece. [24]They said therefore among themselves, "Let us not tear it, but cast lots for it, whose it shall be," that the Scripture might be fulfilled which says:

19:16 [a]NU-Text omits *and led Him away.*

"They divided My garments among them,
And for My clothing they cast lots."[a]

Therefore the soldiers did these things.

Behold Your Mother

[25]Now there stood by the cross of Jesus His mother, and His mother's sister, Mary the *wife* of Clopas, and Mary Magdalene. [26]When Jesus therefore saw His mother, and the disciple whom He loved standing by, He said to His mother, "Woman, behold your son!" [27]Then He said to the disciple, "Behold your mother!" And from that hour that disciple took her to his own *home.*

It Is Finished

[28]After this, Jesus, knowing[a] that all things were now accomplished, that the Scripture might be fulfilled, said, "I thirst!" [29]Now a vessel full of sour wine was sitting there; and they filled a sponge with sour wine, put *it* on hyssop, and put *it* to His mouth. [30]So when Jesus had received the sour wine, He said, "It is finished!" And bowing His head, He gave up His spirit.

Jesus' Side Is Pierced

[31]Therefore, because it was the Preparation *Day,* that the bodies should not remain on the cross on the Sabbath (for that Sabbath was a high day), the

---

19:24 [a]Psalm 22:18   19:28 [a]M-Text reads *seeing.*

Jews asked Pilate that their legs might be broken, and *that* they might be taken away. ³²Then the soldiers came and broke the legs of the first and of the other who was crucified with Him. ³³But when they came to Jesus and saw that He was already dead, they did not break His legs. ³⁴But one of the soldiers pierced His side with a spear, and immediately blood and water came out. ³⁵And he who has seen has testified, and his testimony is true; and he knows that he is telling the truth, so that you may believe. ³⁶For these things were done that the Scripture should be fulfilled, *"Not one of His bones shall be broken."*[a] ³⁷And again another Scripture says, *"They shall look on Him whom they pierced."*[a]

Jesus Buried in Joseph's Tomb

³⁸After this, Joseph of Arimathea, being a disciple of Jesus, but secretly, for fear of the Jews, asked Pilate that he might take away the body of Jesus; and Pilate gave *him* permission. So he came and took the body of Jesus. ³⁹And Nicodemus, who at first came to Jesus by night, also came, bringing a mixture of myrrh and aloes, about a hundred pounds. ⁴⁰Then they took the body of Jesus, and bound it in strips of linen with the spices, as the custom of the Jews is to bury. ⁴¹Now in the place where He was crucified there was a

---

19:36 [a]Exodus 12:46; Numbers 9:12; Psalm 34:20
19:37 [a]Zechariah 12:10

garden, and in the garden a new tomb in which no one had yet been laid. ⁴²So there they laid Jesus, because of the Jews' Preparation *Day,* for the tomb was nearby.

The Empty Tomb

20 Now the first *day* of the week Mary Magdalene went to the tomb early, while it was still dark, and saw *that* the stone had been taken away from the tomb. ²Then she ran and came to Simon Peter, and to the other disciple, whom Jesus loved, and said to them, "They have taken away the Lord out of the tomb, and we do not know where they have laid Him."

³Peter therefore went out, and the other disciple, and were going to the tomb. ⁴So they both ran together, and the other disciple outran Peter and came to the tomb first. ⁵And he, stooping down and looking in, saw the linen cloths lying *there;* yet he did not go in. ⁶Then Simon Peter came, following him, and went into the tomb; and he saw the linen cloths lying *there,* ⁷and the handkerchief that had been around His head, not lying with the linen cloths, but folded together in a place by itself. ⁸Then the other disciple, who came to the tomb first, went in also; and he saw and believed. ⁹For as yet they did not know the Scripture, that He must rise again from the dead. ¹⁰Then the disciples went away again to their own homes.

Mary Magdalene Sees
the Risen Lord

¹¹But Mary stood outside by the tomb weeping, and as she wept she stooped down *and looked* into the tomb. ¹²And she saw two angels in white sitting, one at the head and the other at the feet, where the body of Jesus had lain. ¹³Then they said to her, "Woman, why are you weeping?"

She said to them, "Because they have taken away my Lord, and I do not know where they have laid Him."

¹⁴Now when she had said this, she turned around and saw Jesus standing *there,* and did not know that it was Jesus. ¹⁵Jesus said to her, "Woman, why are you weeping? Whom are you seeking?"

She, supposing Him to be the gardener, said to Him, "Sir, if You have carried Him away, tell me where You have laid Him, and I will take Him away."

¹⁶Jesus said to her, "Mary!"

She turned and said to Him,ᵃ "Rabboni!" (which is to say, Teacher).

¹⁷Jesus said to her, "Do not cling to Me, for I have not yet ascended to My Father; but go to My brethren and say to them, 'I am ascending to My Father and your Father, and *to* My God and your God.' "

¹⁸Mary Magdalene came and told the disciples that she had seen the Lord,ᵃ and *that* He had spoken these

20:16 ᵃNU-Text adds *in Hebrew.*   20:18 ᵃNU-Text reads *disciples, "I have seen the Lord," . . .*

things to her.

The Apostles Commissioned

[19]Then, the same day at evening, being the first *day* of the week, when the doors were shut where the disciples were assembled,[a] for fear of the Jews, Jesus came and stood in the midst, and said to them, "Peace *be* with you." [20]When He had said this, He showed them *His* hands and His side. Then the disciples were glad when they saw the Lord.

[21]So Jesus said to them again, "Peace to you! As the Father has sent Me, I also send you." [22]And when He had said this, He breathed on *them,* and said to them, "Receive the Holy Spirit. [23]If you forgive the sins of any, they are forgiven them; if you retain the *sins* of any, they are retained."

Seeing and Believing

[24]Now Thomas, called the Twin, one of the twelve, was not with them when Jesus came. [25]The other disciples therefore said to him, "We have seen the Lord."

So he said to them, "Unless I see in His hands the print of the nails, and put my finger into the print of the nails, and put my hand into His side, I will not believe."

[26]And after eight days His disciples were again inside, and Thomas with them. Jesus came, the doors being shut,

20:19 [a]NU-Text omits *assembled.*

and stood in the midst, and said, "Peace to you!" [27]Then He said to Thomas, "Reach your finger here, and look at My hands; and reach your hand *here,* and put *it* into My side. Do not be unbelieving, but believing."

[28]And Thomas answered and said to Him, "My Lord and my God!"

[29]Jesus said to him, "Thomas,[a] because you have seen Me, you have believed. Blessed *are* those who have not seen and *yet* have believed."

That You May Believe

[30]And truly Jesus did many other signs in the presence of His disciples, which are not written in this book; [31]but these are written that you may believe that Jesus is the Christ, the Son of God, and that believing you may have life in His name.

Breakfast by the Sea

21 After these things Jesus showed Himself again to the disciples at the Sea of Tiberias, and in this way He showed *Himself:* [2]Simon Peter, Thomas called the Twin, Nathanael of Cana in Galilee, the *sons* of Zebedee, and two others of His disciples were together. [3]Simon Peter said to them, "I am going fishing."

They said to him, "We are going with you also." They went out and immediately[a] got into the boat, and that

---

20:29 [a]NU-Text and M-Text omit *Thomas.*   21:3 [a]NU-Text omits *immediately.*

night they caught nothing. [4]But when the morning had now come, Jesus stood on the shore; yet the disciples did not know that it was Jesus. [5]Then Jesus said to them, "Children, have you any food?"

They answered Him, "No."

[6]And He said to them, "Cast the net on the right side of the boat, and you will find *some*." So they cast, and now they were not able to draw it in because of the multitude of fish.

[7]Therefore that disciple whom Jesus loved said to Peter, "It is the Lord!" Now when Simon Peter heard that it was the Lord, he put on *his* outer garment (for he had removed it), and plunged into the sea. [8]But the other disciples came in the little boat (for they were not far from land, but about two hundred cubits), dragging the net with fish. [9]Then, as soon as they had come to land, they saw a fire of coals there, and fish laid on it, and bread. [10]Jesus said to them, "Bring some of the fish which you have just caught."

[11]Simon Peter went up and dragged the net to land, full of large fish, one hundred and fifty-three; and although there were so many, the net was not broken. [12]Jesus said to them, "Come *and* eat breakfast." Yet none of the disciples dared ask Him, "Who are You?" —knowing that it was the Lord. [13]Jesus then came and took the bread and gave it to them, and likewise the fish.

¹⁴This *is* now the third time Jesus showed Himself to His disciples after He was raised from the dead.

Jesus Restores Peter

¹⁵So when they had eaten breakfast, Jesus said to Simon Peter, "Simon, *son of* Jonah,ᵃ do you love Me more than these?"

He said to Him, "Yes, Lord; You know that I love You."

He said to him, "Feed My lambs."

¹⁶He said to him again a second time, "Simon, *son of* Jonah,ᵃ do you love Me?"

He said to Him, "Yes, Lord; You know that I love You."

He said to him, "Tend My sheep."

¹⁷He said to him the third time, "Simon, *son of* Jonah,ᵃ do you love Me?" Peter was grieved because He said to him the third time, "Do you love Me?"

And he said to Him, "Lord, You know all things; You know that I love You."

Jesus said to him, "Feed My sheep. ¹⁸Most assuredly, I say to you, when you were younger, you girded yourself and walked where you wished; but when you are old, you will stretch out your hands, and another will gird you and carry *you* where you do not wish."

¹⁹This He spoke, signifying by what death he would glorify God. And when He had spoken this, He said to him, "Follow Me."

21:15 ᵃNU-Text reads *John.*   21:16 ᵃNU-Text reads *John.*
21:17 ᵃNU-Text reads *John.*

The Beloved Disciple
and His Book

[20]Then Peter, turning around, saw the disciple whom Jesus loved following, who also had leaned on His breast at the supper, and said, "Lord, who is the one who betrays You?" [21]Peter, seeing him, said to Jesus, "But Lord, what *about* this man?"

[22]Jesus said to him, "If I will that he remain till I come, what *is that* to you? You follow Me."

[23]Then this saying went out among the brethren that this disciple would not die. Yet Jesus did not say to him that he would not die, but, "If I will that he remain till I come, what *is that* to you?"

[24]This is the disciple who testifies of these things, and wrote these things; and we know that his testimony is true.

[25]And there are also many other things that Jesus did, which if they were written one by one, I suppose that even the world itself could not contain the books that would be written. Amen.

The Uniqueness of Jesus

The words "believe" and "believing" are mentioned 90 times in the Gospel of John. In his Gospel, which provides just a glimpse of the life of Jesus of Nazareth, John aims to show that Jesus was not merely a good moral teacher. The purpose of John's Gospel is to convince you to *believe* that Jesus is the promised Messiah, God in human flesh, and that by *believing* that Jesus is the Christ, the Son of God, you may have life in His name (John 20:30,31).

Signs Jesus Is God

If God came to earth, how would we recognize Him? It's noteworthy that no founder of any other religion ever claimed to be God. Only Jesus claimed to be God incarnate—and He backed it up with evidences of His deity. (Unless otherwise noted, the verses below are from the Gospel of John.)

1) He exhibited power over nature: turning water into wine (2:6–10); feeding 5,000 with five loaves and two fish (6:5–14); walking on water (6:16–21); and enabling a miraculous catch of fish (21:3–6,11). It is no big thing for Jesus as the Creator to have dominion over His creation. The time will come when He will exercise His dominion over all of humanity. Give Him dominion over your life in the Day of His grace, before He takes it in the Day of His wrath.

2) He exhibited power over disease: healing the nobleman's son who was near death (4:46–54); healing a man who'd been infirm for 38 years (5:5–9); and restoring the sight of a man born blind (9:1–7,32–33). All sinners lay as feeble, fragile, and frail folk, helpless and hopeless, pathetically paralyzed by the devil— "taken captive to do his will" until they respond in faith to Jesus. They are on a deathbed of sin with no one able to help them, until they hear the voice of the Son of God. As with the infirm man, those who turn from their sin He will make whole.

3) He exhibited power over death, raising from the grave a man who'd been dead four days (11:38–44). Just as His voice brought Lazarus from the grave, His voice will bring all the dead from their graves at the resurrection.

4) He had unparalleled wisdom (6:68; 7:14,15; 7:45,46; 10:19–21). It was rightly said of Jesus, "No man ever spoke like this Man!" (7:46). The dichotomy is that either Jesus was mad or He was God. If He was insane, then close this book and forget Him. However, you have the same dilemma as those who heard Him and saw His supernatural works. Can a madman open the eyes of the blind? Our most brilliant doctors don't know how to open the eyes of one born blind. Does a madman have gracious words pour from His lips? We are therefore left with the conclusion that this Man must be from God as He claimed, and His words must be true. The eternal implications are sobering.

5) He was uniquely without sin (8:46; 18:38; 19:4,6). The Bible says that Jesus "knew no sin" (2 Cor. 5:21), that He was "in all points tempted as we are, yet without sin" (Heb. 4:15), and that He "committed no sin, nor was guile found in His mouth" (1 Pet. 2:22). Even Jesus' enemies could find nothing to pin on Him. He was a perfect, sinless sacrifice for our sins: "He appeared in order to take away sins; and in Him there is no sin" (1 John 3:5).

6) He was omniscient, knowing men's thoughts as well as the future (2:24; 4:17,18,39; 6:64,70–71; 11:14; 13:38; 16:20). In John 16:20 Jesus speaks of the horror of the cross and the unspeakable joy of the resurrection, graphically describing future events—something He continually did. The best of humanity cannot tell what the future holds. We can't even accurately predict tomorrow's weather, let alone events that will take place in the future. In addition, Jesus knows every thought of your heart and your secret sins. Nothing is hidden from His eyes. That will be a comforting thought if you have peace with Him through the cross, and a terrifying one if you don't.

7) He predicted His own death and resurrection (2:18–22; 10:17,18; 12:23–28). Jesus taught His disciples repeatedly of His upcoming death—in detail—and that He would rise from the grave three days later and return to the Father in Heaven. He told them, "Behold, we are going up to Jerusalem, and the Son of Man will be betrayed to the chief priests and to the scribes; and they will condemn Him to death, and deliver Him to the Gentiles to mock and to scourge and to crucify. And the third day He will rise again" (Matt.

20:18,19). His very purpose in coming to earth was to give His life as a ransom for sin: "but now, once at the end of the ages, He has appeared to put away sin by the sacrifice of Himself" (Heb. 9:26).

8) After His resurrection He was seen alive by Mary Magdalene (20:11–18); the disciples without Thomas (20:19,20); the disciples with Thomas (20:24–29); seven of the disciples (21:1–14). These were not "hallucinations" or brief sightings—Jesus ate, drank, and spoke at length with His disciples. Jesus appeared at least 11 times over a 40-day period, and to over 500 eyewitnesses! In writing of this amazing eyewitness testimony, the apostle Paul noted that most of them "remain to the present" (1 Cor. 15:3–7). With witnesses still alive for cross-examination, skeptics could have easily verified the truth of the claim.

Dr. Simon Greenleaf, a founder of Harvard Law School, was one of the greatest legal minds in this country. He concluded that the resurrection of Christ was one of the best supported events in history, according to the laws of legal evidence used in court. In fact, Greenleaf was so convinced by the overwhelming evidence, he committed his life to Christ!

Names Applied to Jesus

The Word of God (1:1,14). The book of Genesis tells us that in the beginning God created everything by His word. He spoke, and it was done. He said, "Let there be light," and there was light. That creative Word became flesh in Jesus of Nazareth. That's why His word was with power, and

the dead came back to life when He spoke
to them (see John 11). When we trust in
Jesus, we are "born again...through the
word of God which lives and abides forever" (1 Pet. 1:23).

The Son of God (1:34; 9:35–37; 10:36;
19:7). There is only one true God, the Creator of heaven and earth, who the Bible
teaches is Triune by nature. He exists eter-
nally as Father, Son, and Holy Spirit—one
God in three divine, co-equal Persons.
Scripture reveals that Jesus Christ, God the
Son, was preexistent before He was manifest in human form: "When the fullness of
the time had come, God sent forth His
Son, born of a woman, born under the
law..." (Gal. 4:4). Jesus is called "the Son
of God" 37 times in the New Testament
and is referred to as "His [God's] Son" or
"the Son" more than twice as many times.

The Lamb of God (1:29,36). When the
Israelites were slaves in Egypt, God told
them to take the blood of a spotless lamb
and put it on the doorposts of their homes.
As He was bringing judgment upon the
Egyptians, when He saw the blood, His
judgment would pass over those in the
house. (The Jewish Passover commemo-
rates this event.) This is a picture of what
God would eventually do through the
coming Messiah. Jesus of Nazareth was
the perfect Lamb provided by God who
was slain to take away the sin of the
world: "You were not redeemed with cor-
ruptible things,...but with the precious
blood of Christ, as of a lamb without
blemish and without spot" (1 Pet.
1:18,19). The judgment of God passes

over all who trust in Jesus' shed blood.

The Son of Man (3:14; 5:27; 6:27; 8:28). In the Old Testament, the title "Son of Man" was a designation for the Messiah. The Book of Daniel predicted that the Son of Man would inherit God's everlasting kingdom (Dan. 7:13,14). "The Son of Man" was used exclusively by Jesus to refer to Himself to emphasize His humanity.

The Messiah/Christ (4:25,26; 4:42; 11:27). Messiah means "anointed one" (the Greek equivalent is "Christ"). Jesus of Nazareth claimed to be the Messiah, the great Deliverer who was promised in the Scriptures. The Bible tells us the Christ would suffer, die, and be raised from the dead, and even tells us the timing of His arrival (Dan. 9:25).

The 7 "I AM" Statements

In these seven "I AM" statements, Jesus was affirming that He was God manifest in the flesh. He is the Great "I AM," the Eternal One who revealed Himself to Moses in the burning bush (Exod. 3:14). Jesus said, " I am . . .":

The Door (10:7,9). There are many religions, each promising to be a door to the afterlife. But there is only entrance to the kingdom of Heaven. Jesus of Nazareth is the Messiah—the Door that leads to immortality, the only antidote to death. The door of eternal salvation is open to all who trust in Him.

The Good Shepherd (10:11–16; 10:27, 28). Centuries earlier, King David had written that the Lord was his shepherd, and now that Shepherd had become flesh. Here is a continuance of the most famous of psalms, Psalm 23. This was the "Great Shepherd" Himself (Heb. 13:20), who takes away the "want" of the covetous human heart. He was the path of righteousness, who brought light to the valley of the shadow of death. Here was the Bread of Life, placed by God on a table in the presence of our enemies. Heaven's cup "ran over," and brought the Father's goodness and mercy to us, so that we might dwell in the House of the Lord forever.

The Bread of Life (6:32–35; 6:48; 6:51, 58). Bread is the staple of this life on earth. Shortly after miraculously feeding the 5,000, Jesus calls Himself the staple of eternal life. He was not advocating cannibalism (that we should eat His flesh), but was speaking in a spiritual sense. Just as we need to eat and drink in order to live, so we must "eat" the Bread of Life (John 6:48,51) and "drink" His "blood, which is shed for you" (Luke 22:20) in order to have spiritual life. Unless we trust in Christ, relying on Him daily for our life-sustaining nourishment, we have no life in us and remain dead in our sins.

The Light of the World (1:7–9; 8:12; 9:5). Jesus is the Light of the world, and all who trust in Him will not abide in darkness. Just after saying this, He gave sight to one who lived in darkness—a man born blind. Think of how the world lives in spiritual darkness: people don't know where they came from, they don't know the future, and they have no idea what causes death or what will happen to them after they die. They sit in the dark shadow of death, waiting for death to come for them. The tragedy is that they are willfully ignorant. They will not come to the Light that they might have life (5:40).

The Resurrection and the Life (11:25, 26). You are a living being. Your life (your soul) is invisible. A doctor may one day pronounce you dead when your life has left your body, but he won't see your life pass into eternity. Jesus is the source of that life, and He alone has the power to raise the dead and grant eternal life. To prove He is "the resurrection and the life," immediately after making this statement Jesus raised Lazarus from the dead. One day He will raise you too: "All who are in the graves will hear His voice and come forth—those who have done good, to the resurrection of life, and those who have done evil, to the resurrection of condemnation" (5:28,29).

The Way, the Truth, and the Life (14:6). Other religions claim there are many ways to God; Jesus claims to be *the* (only) Way. Many assert there is no absolute truth, or that everyone has their own truth; Jesus claims to be *the* Truth. Jesus continually made the incredible claim that He was the very source of life. The Bible says of Jesus, "In Him was life," "Christ, who is our life," and "He who has the Son has life." So those who reject the truth that Jesus Christ is the only way to God reject the most valuable thing in the universe: eternal life.

The True Vine (15:1–6). We are but dead branches unless we have vital union with the life-giving Vine. It is His life flowing through us that enables us to bear fruit. Certain "fruits" should be evident in the lives of those who are in Christ: the fruit of repentance, holiness, praise, thanksgiving, and the fruit of the Spirit—love, joy, peace, longsuffering, kindness, goodness, faithfulness, gentleness, and self-control (Gal. 5:22).

Jesus Is Equal to God the Father

Jesus repeatedly said He is God manifest in human form. This is the teaching of the Bible: "And without controversy great is the mystery of godliness: God was manifested in the flesh, justified in the Spirit, seen by angels, preached among the Gentiles, believed on in the world, received up in glory" (1 Tim. 3:16). The Bible calls Jesus "the image of the invisible God" (Col. 1:15).

Jesus claimed that:

- **He and the Father are one** (5:18; 10:30; 17:11,21,22). Jesus makes the incredible statement that He and the Father are one. How can the two be one? It has been rightly said that when God, the upholder of the universe, became a Man, He didn't cease to be the upholder of the universe. He created for Himself a human body and then filled that body as a hand fills a glove. Scripture says that "it pleased the Father that in Him [Jesus] all the fullness should dwell" (Col. 1:19).

- To know Him is to know God (8:19; 14:7).

- To see Him is to see God (12:45; 14:9).

- To believe in Him is to believe in God (12:44; 14:1).
- To honor Him is to honor God (5:23).
- To hate Him is to hate God (15:23).

Jesus Fulfilled All the Prophecies of the Savior

Over 25 percent of the Bible contains specific predictive prophecies that have been literally fulfilled. This is true of no other book in the world. And it is a sure sign of its divine origin.

God said He would send someone to redeem mankind from sin, and He wanted there to be no mistake about who that Person would be. There are over three hundred prophecies that tell of the ancestry, birth, life, ministry, death, resurrection, and ascension of Jesus of Nazareth. All have been literally fulfilled to the smallest detail. Here are just a few of the prophecies of Jesus, with their fulfillment from the Gospel of John in parentheses:

- God will send His Son: Isa. 7:14; 9:6 ("Immanuel" is translated "God with us.") (fulfilled: John 1:1,14).
- The Messiah will be despised and rejected by men: Isa. 53:3 (1:10,11).
- God will send a messenger before the Messiah: Isa. 40:3 (1:23).
- The Messiah will pay our sin debt: Isa. 53:10,12 (1:29).
- The Spirit of God will be upon Him: Isa. 11:2 (1:32).
- The Messiah will come at a specific time: Dan. 9:25 (4:25,26).

- God will raise up a Prophet like Moses: Deut. 18:15 (6:14).

- Christ will be born in Bethlehem: Micah 5:2 (7:42).

- The Messiah will enter Jerusalem triumphantly: Psa. 118:26 (12:12,13).

- He will enter Jerusalem on a donkey's colt: Zech. 9:9 (12:14–16).

- Many in Israel will not believe in Him: Isa. 53:1 (12:37,38).

- He will speak what God commands: Deut. 18:18 (12:49).

- One who eats bread with the Messiah will betray Him: Psa. 41:9 (13:18,19, 21,26).

- The Messiah will be hated without a cause: Psa. 69:4 (15:25).

- His persecutors will strike Him: Isa. 50:6 (18:22; 19:1–3).

- He will be silent as He is interrogated: Isa. 53:7 (19:9).

- His hands and feet will be pierced: Psa. 22:16,17 (19:18).

- They will cast lots for His clothing: Psa. 22:18 (19:23,24).

- He would thirst on the cross: Psa. 22:15 (19:28).

- None of His bones will be broken: Exod. 12:46; Num. 9:12; Psa. 34:20 (19:33, 36). Jesus is the sacrificial Lamb (John 1:29). Just as the Passover lamb was not to have any bones broken, neither did Jesus, the Lamb of God who was slain to take away the sin of the world.

- The Messiah will be pierced: Zech. 12:10 (19:34,37; 20:27).

- He will be buried in a rich man's tomb: Isa. 53:9 (19:38–42).

Others Bore Witness to Jesus' Deity

God provided all the evidence we would need to recognize the Savior He promised to send. John's Gospel is filled with eyewitness testimony regarding "that which was from the beginning, which we have *heard*, which we have *seen* with our eyes, which we have *looked upon*, and our hands have *handled*, concerning the Word of life..." (1 John 1:13). The following is a small sampling of those who had firsthand experiences with Jesus of Nazareth and bear witness that He is the Son of God:

- John the Baptist (1;7,8; 1:15,32; 5:32, 33; 10:41,42)
- The Holy Spirit (1:32,33)
- The Law & the Prophets (1:45)
- Philip (1:45)
- Nathanael (1:49)
- Scriptures (5:39,46,47)
- The disciples (2:11; 6:14; 6:68,69; 20:28)
- Martha (11:27)
- Samaritans (4:29–42)
- Jesus' works (3:2; 5:36; 6:14; 7:31; 10:21,25; 10:36–38)
- The Father (5:37; 8:18; 12:27–29; see also Luke 3:22)

Jesus' Unique Claims

As stated earlier, Jesus was either God in human form or a crackpot. There is no middle ground. Here are a few of the things He claimed were true of Him:

- **He is preexistent/eternal** (1:1–3; 8:58; 17:5; 17:24). Jesus declared that He not only existed before Abraham, He existed before the creation of the universe. He was with the Father before the world came into existence, and the Father loved Him before the foundation of the world.

- **He created the universe** (1:3,10). Scripture says "by Him all things were created that are in heaven and that are on earth, visible and invisible, whether thrones or dominions or principalities or powers. All things were created through Him and for Him" (Col. 1:16).

- **He came from Heaven** (3:13,31; 6:38,51; 7:29; 8:23,42). Jesus repeatedly said that He had come down from Heaven. He stated, "I am from above ...I am not of this world," and "I proceeded forth and came from God."

- **He gives eternal life** (3:14–16; 3:36; 4:13,14; 5:21,24,25; 6:27,40,47; 8:51; 10:27,28; 17:2,3; 20:31). He claimed that He had the ability to grant everlasting life to all who trust in Him.

- **He has authority over all flesh** (3:35; 17:1,2). Jesus stated, "All authority has been given to Me in heaven and on earth" (Matt. 28:18).

- **He will raise the dead** (5:25; 5:28,29; 6:39,40; 6:54; 11:25). The day is coming when the dead will hear the voice of the Son of God, and billions who have died will be raised to stand before Him in judgment.

- **He will judge mankind** (5:22–27; 9:39). Jesus was ordained by God to be Judge of the living and the dead (Acts 10:42). God "now commands all men everywhere to repent, because He has appointed a day on which He will judge the world in righteousness by the Man whom He has ordained. He has given assurance of this to all by raising Him from the dead" (Acts 17:30,31).

- **Those who don't believe are condemned** (3:18,19; 3:36; 8:24). You are justly condemned by God's Law and are under His wrath. You can face the merciless wrath of the Law and spend eternity in Hell, or you can repent of your sins, fall at the feet of Jesus Christ, and trust in His blood and His wonderful mercy to save you.

- **He will reveal Himself to you** (14:21,23; 17:3). This is the ultimate challenge to any skeptic. Jesus promises that He and the Father will reveal themselves to all who love and obey Him. Read that promise again: "He who has My commandments and keeps them, it is he who loves Me. And he who loves Me will be loved by My Father, and I will love him and manifest Myself to him." Either it is true or it isn't. The proof of the pudding is in the tasting. The Bible tells us to "taste and see that the Lord is good" (Psa. 34:8).

  Your bluff is being called. Stop analyzing the pudding; taste it. If you obey the words of Jesus (to repent and trust in Him), the invisible God of creation will reveal Himself to you. Please, do that today; you may not have tomorrow.

Resources

If you have not yet placed your trust in Jesus Christ and would like additional information, please feel free to visit Living Waters.com and check out our resources. The following items may be especially helpful to you:

How to Know God Exists: Scientific

Proof of God. Clear evidences for His existence will convince you that belief in God is reasonable and rational—a matter of fact and not faith.

Made In Heaven. Discover how the most innovative ideas of modern human ingenuity are actually features borrowed from the amazing work of God in creation.

Scientific Facts in the Bible. Most people don't know that the Bible contains a wealth of incredible scientific, medical, and prophetic facts. The implications are mind-boggling.

See our YouTube channel (youtube.com/ livingwaters) to watch free movies such as "Evolution vs. God," "The Atheist Delusion," "Crazy Bible," as well as thousands of other fascinating videos.

For Christians

Please visit our website where you can sign up for our free weekly e-mail update. To learn how to share your faith the way Jesus did, see these helpful resources:

- *The Evidence Study Bible*

- "Hell's Best Kept Secret" and "True & False Conversion" (listen to these vital messages free at LivingWaters.com)

- *God Has a Wonderful Plan for Your Life: The Myth of the Modern Message* (our most important book)

- "The Way of the Master" Basic & Intermediate Training Courses (DVD)

- "Tough Questions" Apologetics Study

- *What Did Jesus Do?*

- *How to Bring Your Children to Christ . . . & Keep Them There*

- *Out of the Comfort Zone*

- *The Word on the Street: How to Share the Gospel in the Open Air*

You can gain further insights by watching the weekly TV program *Way of the Master* (WayoftheMaster.com), as well as countless videos on our LivingWaters YouTube channel, with over 160,000,000 views.

For more resources, visit **Living Waters.com**, call 800-437-1893, or write to: Living Waters Publications, P.O. Box 1172, Bellflower, CA 90707.